A DOG OWNER'S GUIDE TO
GERMAN SHEPHERD DOGS

a Salamander book

Published by Salamander Books Limited
LONDON • NEW YORK

A DOG OWNER'S GUIDE TO

GERMAN SHEPHERD DOGS

Roy and Clarissa Allan
Photographs by Marc Henrie

A Salamander Book

© 1988 Salamander Books Ltd
52 Bedford Row
London WC1R 4LR

ISBN 0-86101-344-1

Distributed in the UK by Hodder and Stoughton Services, PO Box 6, Mill Road, Dunton Green, Sevenoaks, Kent TN13 2XX.

Credits

Editor: Tony Hall
Designer: Philip Gorton
Photographs: Marc Henrie
Illustrations: Ray Hutchins
Colour origination: Rodney Howe Ltd
Typesetting: The Old Mill
Printed in Portugal

Contents

Authors

Roy Allan: Has owned GSDs for 40 years. Started showing in 1958 and breeding in 1963. Together with Clarissa has bred 8 British and 9 overseas champions. Began judging breed in 1969, at championship level since 1973; approved SV judge since 1982. Has judged internationally for many years. For four years Instructor and Examiner for the GSD League Judges Training Scheme. He is currently President of the British German Shepherd Dog Training Club.

Clarissa Allan: Owned first GSD in 1944. Started working and showing GSDs in 1958; started breeding 1963. International judge; judged first championship show 1968; approved SV judge 1982. With Roy, one of the Founder Trustees of the GSD Improvement Foundation. League Council member since 1972. Founder, Instructor and Examiner for the League Judges Training Scheme. In charge of League Assessments. Has competed in working trials and obedience with champion GSDs.

Veterinary consultant

Trevor Turner qualified from the Royal Veterinary College, London, in 1958 and within a few months had set up a small animal practice at his home in Northolt, near London. He now runs an extensive small animal hospital. Trevor has always owned dogs and cats in multiplicity. Litters are planned and bred on an occasional basis.

An active member of many veterinary associations and past president of some, Trevor writes and speaks widely on a variety of topics connected with small animal practice. He believes that the role of the vet involves not only treatment of the patient but also intelligible communication with the owners, who should always feel free to question and discuss problems with the veterinarian.

US consultant

Hal Sundstrom, as president of Halamar Inc, publishers, of North Virginia, has been editing and publishing magazines on travel and pure-bred dogs since 1972. He is the recipient of six national writing and public excellence awards from the Dog Writer's Association of America, of which he is now president, and he is a past member of the Collie Club of America. He is now a delegate to the AKC representing the Collie Club of America.

Hal has an extensive background and enormous experience in the dog world as a breeder/handler/exhibitor, match and sweeps judge, officer and director of specialty and all-breed clubs, show and symposium chairman, and officer of the Arizona and Hawaii Councils of Dog Clubs.

Photographer

Marc Henrie began his career as a Stills man at the famous Ealing Film Studios in London. He then moved to Hollywood where he worked for MGM, RKO, Paramount and Warner Brothers.

After he had returned to England, Marc specialised in photographing dogs and cats, establishing an international reputation.

He has won numerous photographic awards, most recently the Kodak Award for the Best Animal Photograph and the Neal Foundation Award for Outstanding Photography of Animal Behaviour.

Marc is married to ex-ballet dancer, Fiona Henrie. They live in West London with their daughter Fleur, two King Charles Cavalier Spaniels and a cat called Topaz.

Authors' acknowledgements

We wish to thank the SV in Augsburg, West Germany for allowing us to print archive material and to reproduce pictures of Sieger Uran v. Wildsteigerland and Sieger Quando v. Arminius. We also thank the many people who contributed photographic material to us. For permission to print photos used in the book we give grateful acknowledgement to: Mr & Mrs Paul Bradley; Mr & Mrs John Young; Mr & Mrs Peter Brown; Mr & Mrs David Hall; Mrs Sylvia Harrison; Mr & Mrs Laurie Green; Mr & Mrs Jim Bellfield; also photographs by Mr John Berry and Mr Eric Stoddart. We are also grateful for the help given to us by 'Royal Canin'. Our eternal thanks go to Mrs 'Steve' Wooldridge for typing and reading the proofs. We don't know how we would have managed otherwise. Lastly we thank the GSD League of Great Britain for allowing us to print the Standard for the breed.

Cover photograph: Ch: Shootersway Lido, Best GSD at Crufts 1987.

Introduction

When we were asked to write this book, we felt highly honoured, but at first unsure as to how we should tackle such a subject.

Many good books have been written both for the first-time Shepherd owner and for the more experienced enthusiast. Few, however, have been aimed at the type of owner who has gained so much pleasure from the versatility of the GSD as a pet that he or she has become determined to make progress towards a deeper and wider understanding of the breed. This has been our own experience with German Shepherds.

Having owned GSDs as pets, we became so enthralled with them that we decided to become more deeply involved with the breed, a decision we have never regretted.

A history

We started showing in 1958 with Shootersway Benedict. It was with this dog that we first tasted the thrill of winning prizes in the show ring. More importantly, however, we learned a lot about the breed in the wider sense, including its special abilities for work.

It was perhaps inevitable after this success that we should decide to start breeding GSDs ourselves. We consequently purchased a bitch: Shootersway Lucretia of Stranmillis.

In the meantime we visited Germany. The dogs we saw there so impressed us that we immediately realised that this was the type of German Shepherd that we wished to produce ourselves: strong, compact, athletic dogs with super characters and temperaments.

When the time came to mate Lucretia, we felt we knew what we wanted, but did not know where we could find the right partner. The popular sire of the time — a dog everyone seemed to be using — did

not produce the qualities we were seeking.

Then suddenly at a show in London we saw a 15-month-old dog, Atstan Impresario (who was later to become a champion). He seemed to our eyes to be the embodiment of the true German Shepherd male. We were thrilled to discover that the kennel from which he came was active in the field of working dogs. We also noted that the results of such a mating would involve line-breeding on the dominant German sire, Lex Preussenblut. Lucretia was duly mated and the litter — our first — was born on 1st February 1963.

The GSD world community

Since then through our travels abroad in connection with German Shepherds, we have met many interesting people and have made a lot of friends. Whatever country you care to visit, as a breeder and lover of the GSD, you will always be made welcome by other enthusiasts.

Over the years we have had a great deal of pleasure and enjoyment from our involvement in the breed. It has given us a life-long interest. The challenge of trying to produce the perfect German Shepherd Dog will always remain with us.

In this book we have given you what we believe to be a firm foundation of information on breeding and working. We hope it will inspire you, as we have been inspired over the years.

Below left: *The adult German Shepherd; alert, intelligent, athletic and strong. A dog well-suited for any role.*

Below: *Space and exercise are essential to the German Shepherd, as is the owner's devotion of time and effort to its welfare.*

Chapter One

A HISTORY OF THE BREED

The SV
Police dogs
The Breed Survey
Utz vom Haus Schütting

Since the dawn of history, man and dog have had a complementary relationship. When man was a hunter, the acute hearing, swiftness of movement and excellent scenting ability of the dog created an ideal partner in seeking out and killing prey. In return for this work the dog received shelter and food.

The defensive as well as the offensive traits in the character of the dog assumed greater importance as man progressed and emerged from his role as hunter to a more settled existence. Man's acquisition of land and stock marked the dawn of the pastoral age in which the dog was to play the part of protector.

Now began the process of specialised breeding, firstly into two main groups of hunting and herding dogs. The many types of herding dogs performed the function of controlling and guarding the flocks as an aid to, and sometimes as a substitute for, the shepherd.

The regional shepherd dogs of Germany had existed for centuries; their type and conformation varied according to the terrain and the movement patterns of the flocks themselves. In the hilly regions of the south, a hardy strain of working dogs developed — large boned with powerful hindquarters and with firm and correct forehand angulation — entirely necessary for movement up and down steep slopes to control the flocks. On the plains of northern Germany, on the other hand, the need was for an athletic, long-striding type of dog, capable of prolonged, tireless trotting over large expanses of terrain, which featured few natural or man-made boundaries. It was on these plains that the concept of the shepherd dog as 'living fence' was first developed; at once to contain the often large flocks, as well as to ward off intruders of whatever kind.

Thuringian shepherds
In Germany in the nineteenth century, interest in the native shepherd breeds grew steadily. The breeders of Württemberg,

themselves mostly shepherds and farmers, looked to the north and in particular to the dogs of Thuringia, to improve ear carriage and coat colour, for it was these characteristics that their own dogs lacked. Especially prized was the wolf-grey colour of the Thuringian shepherd dog, whose outgoing temperament and joy of life was found desirable for introduction into the more sober southern strains. Coats of different textures and lengths were not necessarily confined, however, to particular areas, and so, in spite of later attempts to stabilise coat types, variations still come through including the long-coated German Shepherd Dog of today, so much admired by many lovers of the breed.

THE SV

These activities came to the notice of the 'fanciers' and on the 16th December 1891, the Phylax Society was formed. Support for this quickly dwindled, and in its stead what was to become the largest one-breed society in the world was founded on 22nd April 1899: Der Verein für Deutsche Schäferhunde (SV), whose president was Cavalry Captain Max von Stephanitz. This great and far-sighted man realised that with the arrival of the industrial society, rural life would eventually decline, and that new uses would have to be found for the shepherd dog. He knew that if the breed were to endure he must fix type and thus create a 'national' shepherd dog, a blend of the best characteristics from the regions of north and south. The process had already begun. He was to complete it. Von Stephanitz also realised the weakness of man's nature and the short-comings of human endeavour. He had to devise a system which would not only fix,

---

Right: *Horand v. Grafrath (lying) and Mari v. Grafrath (sitting). As SZ 1 and SZ 2, these were the first two GSDs ever registered.*

but maintain type in the generations to come. He had to ensure, if he were to succeed, that future breeders did not deviate from the path he would set.

Horand von Grafrath

The first 'national' German Shepherd was known as Hektor Linksrhein. Von Stephanitz acquired this dog from the Sparwasser kennels and renamed him under his own kennel prefix: Horand von Grafrath. He was to appear as the first entry in the new SV Breed Register the SZ (Zuchtbuch für Deutsche Schäferhunde). Horand was thus SZ 1. In his famous book *The German Shepherd Dog in Word and Picture,* von Stephanitz wrote as follows. "... for the enthusiasts of that time Horand embodied the fulfilment of their fondest dreams; he was large — from 24-24½ in (61-62cm), height of back ... and even from the point of view of present conditions a very good medium size, with powerful bones, beautiful lines and nobly formed head; clean and sinewy in build, the whole dog was a live wire. His character corresponded to his exterior qualities ... marvellous in his obedient faithfulness to his master; above all, the straight-forward nature of a gentleman with a boundless and irrepressible zest for living ... Horand handed down these wonderful characteristics to his immediate descendants. These still survive today ..."

Hektor von Schwaben

Horand's most famous son was Hektor von Schwaben, SZ 13. He was Sieger, or German Grand Champion, of 1900 and 1901, whose dam was the working bitch Mores-Plieningen from Württemberg, SZ 159 HGH.

From the amorphous strains of regional shepherd dogs and from the joining of the northern and southern types, each contributing its own special qualities, emerged the new 'national' shepherd dog — the German Shepherd Dog.

The Phylax had failed as a breed club because it was not what the 'users' wanted; if it had stayed the course, would the German

Shepherd have become just another 'fanciers' show-dog? At the dawn of the industrial age, when the demand for sheep-herding was in decline, might this newly created wonder-dog have been condemned to become just another non-working dog in the Working Group competition, which is a feature of dog shows in many countries? Where the German Shepherd Dog became well-established a conflict was to develop, especially in English-speaking countries, as to whether the show-type and the working-type should be separated.

Von Stephanitz had no such doubts when he formed the SV. "To breed a German Shepherd Dog is to breed a working-dog", was the basis of his thinking. In Germany this principle has never been abandoned. The top winners at the annual Sieger Show have to pass working tests before being considered for high show awards.

Von Stephanitz created an organisation for the development and control of his beloved breed over which he exercised absolute authority. The SV was able to gain acceptance at the outset because the breeders and 'users' as well as

Above: *Hektor v. Schwaben SZ 13. Son of Horand out of Mores-Plieningen. He united the north and south strains of GSD.*

the 'fanciers', such as they were, totally accepted the aims and principles for the development of the breed. Furthermore they were prepared to accept the imposition of rules which, as the years went by, tended to become more rather than less exacting.

Von Stephanitz evaluated the shepherd dog in the light of new functions and duties which he imagined would eventually take over, but hopefully not replace, the control of flocks. Clearly the most obvious characteristic to exploit was the dog's guarding instinct, recognised from the way in which the shepherd dogs, from time immemorial, had protected the flocks from intrusion and attack. This quality, which the Germans called 'Kampftrieb', means not only the ability but also the *willingness* to protect. The word also implies an active or offensive, as well as a passive or defensive, quality. The SV encouraged its members to develop all the manifold qualities possessed by the German Shepherd breed in readiness for the wide-ranging tasks which lay ahead of it in the future.

POLICE DOGS

An early role for the German Shepherd was that of police dog. As early as 1901 the SV suggested the dog's use as such to the police authorities. Efficiency trials began in 1903. The results were so satisfactory that police administrations in many large towns were persuaded to try out and eventually to adopt the dogs as an integral part of the law enforcement system. The government established a breeding and training centre for police dogs in Grünheide, near Berlin.

In the beginning there was some wariness amongst police chiefs about the use of German Shepherd Dogs as detective or criminal investigation dogs. This class of work called for tracking and searching skills, and it was soon discovered at Grünheide and other training centres that the dog had exceptional skills in the field of nosework. Thus, dogs from the schools began to graduate to operational duties in the security and military police. The fame of Grünheide as the 'hochschule' (high school) of police dog training spread far and wide. Up until the outbreak of World War I, in fact, police contingents came from many countries around the world to return home with fully trained dogs. In this way the basis was laid for police dog sections on an international scale, with the German Shepherd Dog playing an indispensable role in law enforcement which today is taken for granted.

At the outbreak of World War I, the skills of the German Shepherd Dog, which had been fully investigated by the police, were taken up by the military. The acute hearing and scenting ability was invaluable at sentry posts to give warning of enemy attack.

Dog at war
Another characteristic exploited during this period was the dog's love of master. Special training was given to develop the instinct, so that the dog could be employed to send messages 'back home' to trench and dug-out. In this way the invaluable despatch-dog service was created. Moreover, the dog's tracking and searching skills which had been fully developed by the police for criminal detection now began to be adapted to the task of seeking out wounded soldiers on the battlefield. The German Shepherd had become established in the motherland of the breed.

As the breed was gaining recognition, the SV was determined that it should continue as a working breed and that the skills for which the dog had already become famous should not be allowed to languish or fall into disuse. Yet the breeders of working dogs, usually farmers and shepherds, did not keep records in any permanent sense. They tended to lack a feeling for and knowledge of a 'grand design' for breeding concentrating instead on the 'ad hoc' needs of the moment. Without someone like von Stephanitz, it is doubtful whether the amorphous mass of shepherd dogs in Germany, dogs of different size, conformation, coat and character, would ever have been welded into the German Shepherd Dog we know and love today. What he saw so clearly was the need for a Standard for the breed which was sufficiently precise and detailed as to leave little doubt as to its interpretation. This Standard, which was drawn up at the outset, has with few amendments remained an invaluable 'blueprint' for the breeding of the German Shepherd Dog.

WUSV

Since the creation of the WUSV, (The World Union of German Shepherd Dog Clubs), the trend has been for member countries, including those whose mother tongue is English, to persuade the breed and ruling authority in their own lands to adopt the original German Standard for the breed, now known as the WUSV/FCI (International Canine Federation)Standard. This changeover is now virtually complete, except that the United States, although a member country of the WUSV, has not as yet come into line.

Controlled breeding

If the first stage was to establish an exact 'blueprint', the next was to ensure that breeders used only officially approved breeding animals. Breeders of dogs in the English-speaking world cherish their freedom; they take pride, justifiably, in establishing a kennel, breeding what are acclaimed by judges as good dogs, receiving the accolades and eventually taking their place as breed-leaders. Such people may find the concept of controlled breeding and the conformation to a pre-conceived plan somewhat strange and restrictive.

Von Stephanitz, however, felt that the system of entry in the Breed Register purely by show-win, as is the case with the British Kennel Club Stud Book, or the American Register of Merit (ROM), through winning progeny, was unsatisfactory because it was incomplete and could in fact be misleading as a guide to breeding worth. He described the situation in this way: "The demand that only exhibition qualifications should be considered, would have placed the breed on too narrow a basis, and because this really depends on all kinds of contingencies, it accordingly would have given a quite false impression of the 'crème de la crème of the race."

The SV decided that their Stud Book, or rather, Breed Register (Zuchtbuch), should be a record of all existing German Shepherd Dogs together with proof of their origin. It was felt that the information supplied about each dog in the Breed Register would be a valuable

guide for the use of the breeder, especially applied in conjunction with the Breed Survey Book (Körbuch).

THE BREED SURVEY

But what is a Breed Survey Book? What in fact is a breed survey (Körung)?

The first Breed Survey Book of the German Shepherd Dog was issued in Germany in 1922. The following quote is an extract of a review of this publication, compiled from official SV sources.

The first Körbuch of the SV foreshadows extraordinarily important progress for the breed and for its furtherance in general. The comparative figures of the Körbuch are also instructive. . . because they furnish us with such a complete survey as we have had up to now. . . The Körbuch in question contains measurements of the height at wither, of the depth of chest, of the contour of the chest, of the general body length, and of the weight of the body. . . It is only the motto of our breeding 'to breed a German Shepherd Dog is to breed a working dog', that is to be considered, and that is why we should put special value on the correct ratio between height at wither and length of body. The use and work of the German Shepherd Dog require endurance in trotting. For this purpose a rather rectangular, and not a square formation is required . . . According to the correct figures concerning 210 dogs (in the survey) in measurements and in weights, the 'normal' German Shepherd male should, in order to satisfy the requirements of the present time, be produced bodily as follows:

body length approx 71 cms
wither height approx 64.5 cms
excess of length over height
approx 6.5 cms
depth of chest approx 28 cms
chest contour approx 75 cms
weight approx 27.5 kgs

The survey is conducted by the breed-master (Körmeister) who measures, weighs and assesses the dog for conformation and temperament against the Standard. Breeding recommendations are given, as well as warnings. Dogs in Class 1 are those recommended for breeding; dogs in Class 2 are suitable for breeding. To be admitted into Class 1 or Class 2, dogs must be in possession of a working (Schutzhund) qualification and an 'A Stamp' for hips which denotes hips good enough for breeding. Dogs not classified in the breed survey, the results of which are compiled on an annual basis in the Körbuch, are not used for breeding and are discarded as far as the SV system is concerned. Animals two years of age and over are eligible for the breed survey.

Spreading fame
As the breed developed in Germany, its fame spread to the United States and to Britain, and from there to many other countries.

In America no dog of importance was imported until the formation, in 1913, of the German Shepherd Dog Club of America. The following year saw the arrival of Apollo von Hunenstein, who in 1919 was to become US Grand Victor. It was not until after World War I, however, that the breed really took hold.

Soldiers returning from the battlefields of Europe told of the wondrous feats performed by German Shepherds under fire. The escapades of Rin-Tin-Tin and Strongheart, championing the cause of good against evil on the world's cinema screens, stirred the imagination of people everywhere. In 1919 the German Shepherd Dog League of Great Britain (known at first as the Alsatian League and Club of Great Britain) was founded. From 1922 some 60 German Shepherds arrived in Australia. However, by 1929 a ban had been imposed on any further imports. According to the Australian breed authority, the late Walter Reimann, the ban — which was not lifted for 43 years — was due to three main reasons: ignorance and carelessness of individual owners; opposition of some parliamentarians, who were

Below: Utz v. Haus Schütting, the 1929 Sieger. Utz revolutionised the breed and is often called the 'father of the modern GSD'.

breeders of Australian Sheepdogs and, most importantly, the importation of mentally inferior stock — the progeny of dogs which in Germany, "had been expelled from the showrings and their breeding permit cancelled because of bad nerves and unstable temperament and hereditary faults".

The Australian experience should be a salutary lesson to us all; that it is dangerous to use stock that derives from breed survey rejects. It is also dangerous to overlook the enemies of our breed; by behaving irresponsibly with our Shepherds we are merely playing into their hands.

In the early twenties an attempt was made in America to start breed surveys after the German model but with some modifications. Differences in national character took over, however, and individual kennels tended firstly to question and finally to undermine the breed survey concept, which eventually faded into oblivion.

Since the formation of the WUSV, breed surveys have been introduced in many countries outside the SV system, including the United States, Britain and Australia. In these countries, however, the aim has been to provide accurate breed-information rather than to control breeding material.

Whilst the cooperative approach to the breeding of dogs may have been rejected by Americans and indeed other nations in the English-speaking world, individual breeders were nevertheless attempting to lay a firm foundation for the breed. In America, the Fortunate Fields Kennel, for example, made a scientific study of the breed and by blending the very best of German bloodlines in regard to working and conformation, eventually produced Shepherds for every branch of canine endeavour for which their physical and mental qualities made them eminently suitable, especially for the famous 'Seeing Eye' — the centre for guide dogs for the blind at Morristown, New Jersey.

UTZ vom HAUS SCHÜTTING

In Germany, early examples of the breed, such as Roland v. Starkenburg, Sieger 1906 and 1907, and the 1910 Sieger Tell von der Kriminalpolizei, which were somewhat square, rather high on the legs, almost terrier fronted and lacking in hind-angulation, were being replaced by an improved type of dog. The 1920 Sieger Erich von Grafenwerth started a trend towards a deeper bodied dog, less square and with more angulation. Five of his progeny attained championship titles in England. Erich, together with many other fine dogs, was exported to America during this period. Most important is the fact that Erich was the sire of the famous 1925 Sieger Klodo v. Boxberg, whose son, the 1929 Sieger Utz vom Haus Schütting, was to revolutionise the breed. Von Stephanitz considered that Utz demonstrated, "the purest form of an efficient and serviceable shepherd-dog body build, powerful but without too much weight".

The main influence of Utz in Britain was through his son Voss von Bern imported by the Brittas kennel, who also brought in Arno v. Bibliserwald, a grandson of Klodo v. Boxberg, for the purpose of mating to bitches of the Utz line, thus establishing in the British Isles what von Stephanitz referred to as the Klodo/Utz type ie the correct type. It is interesting to note that the great producing sire in the United States, Sieger Pfeffer von Bern, was descended from Voss's litter sister, Vicki von Bern. Pfeffer, together with his half brother, the great Ch. Odin v. Busecker Schloss, were influential in moulding the breed in America.

The cooperation of breeders in Germany and respect for the rules imposed by the SV, worked in

Right: *Quanto v.d. Wienerau. Through his descendants this dog is one of the three 'pillars' of the GSD breed today.*

favour of action to rectify the failings and promote the virtues of particular bloodlines. Regrettably, the lack of policy direction and control in Britain and America resulted in the abuse of freedoms by unscrupulous and ignorant breeders. Whilst Germany kept producing fine stock right until World War II, the breed outside the SV orbit took a downward path in quality and in popularity. It was not until the WUSV was launched in

Above: *Mutz v.d. Pelztierfarm. One of the most influential dogs of today's bloodlines, together with Quanto and Canto v.d. Wienerau.*

the early seventies presided over by the late Dr Christolph Rummel, as an organisation devoted to the improvement of the breed on a world-wide basis, that this downward trend in quality began to be significantly reversed.

Chapter Two

CHOOSING A PUPPY

The purchase
Temperament
Availability
Colour
The Affix

The first consideration before taking steps to choose a puppy is to ask yourself whether the puppy would choose you as an owner! Consider the basic statistics of an adult German Shepherd:

height (male) up to 65cm at the withers

height (female) up to 60cm at the withers

weight (male) very approx 34-39kg

weight (female) very approx 27-36kg

This is a dog of medium size in relation to other breeds, and whilst all puppies are small, attractive and cuddly, it is well to consider whether the German Shepherd as an adult suits your lifestyle and accommodation.

Do you have the time to devote to such an active and intelligent breed?

Will you train your dog in basic obedience to play a responsible role in modern society?

At home, do you have a garden or piece of ground which your dog can regard as its own?

Have you carefully considered the cost, not only of the purchase price of the puppy, but also of accessories such as lead, check-chain, puppy bed and toys?

Other costs will include: feeding, inoculations and possible veterinary treatment; kennel club fees in respect of transfer of ownership; training fees for obedience classes as well as the possible building and upkeep of an outside kennel and run.

Of considerable importance is the need for someone, preferably a member of the family, to be with the puppy during its waking hours for at least the first six months of its life, not only to administer the necessary feeds, but also to offer the puppy companionship. Will the puppy be 'socialised' into the outside world, after inoculations, so that it can come to terms with those beyond the home environment, whether they are human or canine?

THE PURCHASE

Let us suppose you have now made the decision to purchase a puppy. What are the next steps? If you lived in Germany you would almost certainly pay a visit to the local branch (Ortsgruppe) of the SV, where you would be introduced to the breed-warden for the area. You would then be put in touch with breeders who have litters. The breed-warden knows that all the breeders in his area, for whom he acts as adviser, are producing stock to pre-set high standards — standards which are based on selection for type, good hip-status, correct temperament and working capability, including the ability to protect. Haphazard or irresponsible breeding is simply not tolerated and no such stock would obtain registration papers from the SV.

In countries outside the SV system, the position is rather different and much more complicated. In the first place, breeders are responsible only to themselves; as long as they work within the law of the land they can put on to the market whatever they think will sell. The general public will be mainly concerned with a dog as one of a particular breed, and they will judge it on what they can see (the phenotype). It is, unfortunately, the part they cannot see (the genotype) which is the problem area for the prospective buyer. What makes matters worse is the confusion which surrounds the definition of a 'breeder'.

At a basic level, someone with a dog and a bitch, who has produced puppies by the mating of the one with the other, can be called a breeder. The prospective buyer may see an advert in the press offering the puppies of such a mating for sale, often at the current market price. The puppies will then be inspected by the prospective buyer and may look well-reared and appear as normal, healthy examples of the breed. In these circumstances there may be no apparent reason why the puppy should not be purchased, though it is precisely in this way that many puppies *are* purchased, often with disastrous consequences!

The right puppy

How then can the prospective buyer obtain a puppy which is correct to the Standard and healthy in mind and body; a puppy which will develop into a typical German Shepherd without costing a fortune in veterinary expenses? The answer to the question is that where one is dealing with flesh and blood,

no-one can be certain of anything. The breeding of dogs is an art not a science, although today, scientific aids, such as genetic analysis and hip scoring, are being employed on an increasing scale.

In practice, the situation is not as difficult as it might seem. Contact your kennel club for a list of registered breeders. Above all, join the national club for the breed in your country; attend some breed shows and look at the stock

Below: *A four week old sable male puppy in the show position. He is of good type and substance, with a very nice head.*

exhibited. You should also read up on the breed as much as possible. Most breed clubs publish a magazine or newsletter, and in some cases a yearly handbook. Some countries, such as Great Britain, publish weekly newspapers devoted entirely to canine affairs and topics. Do not forget that in many urban areas you will find a local breed club for the German Shepherd whose committee is concerned with providing training in breed and in obedience.

Let us suppose then that you have now obtained a list of likely breed kennels who have, or may have, young stock available for sale. How do you know about the relative merits of the breeders on the list you have been given? You probably have neither the time nor the inclination to visit all the kennels; and even if you did, this might make you more confused than ever when seeing so many puppies. You could always telephone round, this being an essential exercise anyway prior to visiting a kennel, if only to establish the availability of puppies.

Quite clearly, unless you have been especially recommended to a kennel by a friend whose judgement you trust, it will be as well to establish a check-list of essential requirements for a puppy before embarking upon a time-consuming and perhaps expensive visit which may prove abortive. These requirements can be said to be: type, good hip-status, correct temperament and working ability.

A dog of 'good type' is close in all important respects, and is the living embodiment of, the Standard for the breed. If you are interested in a German Shepherd puppy merely as a pet you would be well advised to keep your options open; many breeders started as pet owners themselves.

GOOD HIPS

Good hip-status is necessary in breeding stock, so that puppies bred from such stock are more likely to have good hips, ie hips with good deep sockets and well shaped femur heads. Hip dysplasia, which could be described as a malformation of the hip joints (see Chapter 7), is present to a degree in many large breeds. Contrary to popular belief, German Shepherds are not the worst afflicted. In many countries a facility is provided to enable breeders to have hip X-rays taken and evaluated by experts when stock has reached the age of one year. In America, hips are X-rayed at the age of two years and if found to conform to the standards set by the OFA (Orthopedic Foundation for Animals), a numbered certificate is granted. In Germany, the SV endorse pedigrees with the 'A Stamp' to certify that the particular dog, whose hips have been X-rayed at one year, has met the required standard for breeding. In Great Britain the BVA (British Veterinary Association) issue a score 0-106 — a low score meaning good hips.

You may wonder: why is there all this concern about hips? Anyone who has owned a dog with severe hip dysplasia will tell you about the pain and distress suffered by the poor dog whose hips do not give proper support to the back legs. The condition cannot be diagnosed except by X-ray examination, so you will be well advised to ask the breeder about the hip-status of the sire and dam of the litter in which you may be interested.

TEMPERAMENT

The question of temperament in the German Shepherd is clearly defined in the Standard, which is discussed in Chapter 8. Nevertheless, a degree of subjectivity will always enter into any discussion upon temperament and character.

A recent judges' report on a candidate for best puppy described the puppy, on the one hand, as having a good temperament, whilst the co-judge would not accept the animal at any price, describing it as a 'coward'. A referee had to be called to settle the difference of opinion. If judges can disagree,

Above: *A lively litter ready for play. Judging the temperament of a puppy is difficult, but must be given serious consideration.*

how much more difficult is it for the prospective owner of a German Shepherd puppy to make the right decision! Clearly, before visiting a breeder, point out during your initial telephone discussion how important you regard the question of temperament and see what kind or response you get. Most breeders, proud of their dogs and their characters, will want to show them off.

On arrival you should ask to see all the dogs in the kennel from which you will be able to make an overall assessment. If you are interested in a working dog; if you intend to engage in obedience, tracking, agility or protection work (known often as 'schutzhund'),

then you are strongly advised to contact as many organisations devoted to this class of activity as possible. In this way you should obtain guidance as to those breeders specialising in work as well as conformation. In the context of the working dog, a breeder's credentials and achievements with his or her own breeding are of the utmost importance. Remember, the difference between dogs is not just the ability, but also the desire to work.

27

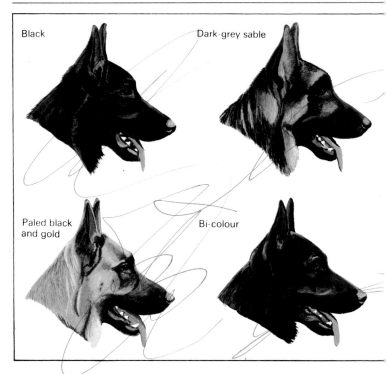

Black

Dark-grey sable

Paled black and gold

Bi-colour

Armed, therefore, with the necessary background information, you are now in a position to make some visits and inspect some litters.

Above: *Six types of head and neck colouration in the adult German Shepherd. These should not be confused with puppy colours.*

Bitch or dog?

Undoubtedly, the first question to be decided upon is whether to go for a male or female. As we have seen, a bitch will be smaller not just in height but in overall size. Naturally, if you want to keep your options open, a female can be your best investment, because she can be bred from. A bitch will come into season on average about every six months, the first season starting usually at about eight or nine months of age. During this period, you will of course have to make arrangements for her to be kept apart from any would-be mates. If it is difficult to achieve this in practice you would be well advised to place the bitch in a boarding-kennel for the three weeks or so until her season ends.

The male German Shepherd, as well as being larger, is also likely to be stronger and more powerful. When it comes to a choice, some trainers believe that the female is more willing to please and is more responsive to training. Some potential owners may also be put off by the male practice of marking territory by urination. Other than these considerations, choosing between a dog and bitch comes down very much to a matter of personal preference.

AVAILABILITY

At this stage you may ask yourself how you would go about selecting a puppy from a litter. In practice, choice works by rotation on a 'first come, first serve' basis. Thus it is as well to consider this question of choice and availability of puppies from any litter.

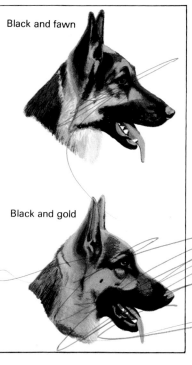

Black and fawn

Black and gold

Most breeders have to devise a form of booking their puppies, so that they will not be left with any. The principle which seems to work best is to take deposits from buyers when the puppies are about four weeks, on the basis of first, second, third and fourth choice, and so on. The buyer will have bought into the litter on the basis of the overall quality, but will not make the actual choice until the puppies can be taken away, say at seven or eight weeks. The choice cannot be made at four weeks because the puppy will grow and therefore change in the following three or four weeks.

Initial enquiries
When making the initial enquiry about a litter which has not long been whelped, find out whether options have been taken up by deposit, and therefore what choice you have. It is annoying to see a large litter of nice puppies running about, only to be told that most of them have been booked. Again, in

practice, it is unlikely that a reasonable breeder will fail to tell you about the choice left available, before you commit yourself to making the journey. If you want a puppy to take away immediately, you may be lucky to be able to view a reasonably sized litter of seven week old puppies from which no bookings have yet been made. The puppies from popular breed kennels may very well be booked quickly and often in advance. In such cases it is always possible to book a puppy from any future litter, subject of course to inspection when the time comes.

The process of booking a puppy at four weeks and collecting at seven weeks creates special problems where distances are very great, because of the need for more than one journey. The way round this would be, after discussion with any understanding breeder, to send your deposit to secure an early choice of a puppy from a litter; on the appointed day for selecting and taking the puppy, and armed with first or second choice, you are really no worse off if the litter is to your liking. If it isn't, then you may be able to transfer the deposit to a later litter, according to whatever arrangements you made with the breeder in the first place.

Last puppies
At this stage it is important to understand, however, that if you are offered puppies from a litter where you do not have first, second or third choice, or where you are told that there are only one or two left unbooked, then you should not assume that these will not be good puppies worthy of your consideration.

The choosing of puppies is subjective, and depends upon what people are looking for: coat length, colour, size, to name only three. There have been many cases where the last puppies in a litter turned out to be the best. Again, consult the breeder about this. State your needs and decide whether it is worth making the trip on the basis of what you have been told.

Remember, no good breeder who values his or her reputation will want to sell you a bad puppy! Furthermore, breeders may reserve puppies, either for their own purposes, such as future breeding requirements, or for possible customers who may want puppies for showing in the breed ring. Either way breeders can't really lose, because if they were to decide not to run on anything themselves, a good puppy of 'show quality' is seldom difficult to place with a suitable buyer. Let us remind ourselves that we are discussing puppies of seven or eight weeks. Older puppies from 6-12 months are a different matter. Such puppies may be of interest to the showing and working enthusiast, rather than to the pet owner. (See also Chapter 8 on showing and the Standard).

PRIORITIES

Having observed and listened to the reactions and comments of potential buyers of puppies and young stock over the quarter-century or so that we have been breeding, our experience of the range of personal priorities has left us with some very strong impressions.

Many people, for example, are looking for a particular colour, say brilliant black and gold or grey-sable. A lot of people like a long-coated Shepherd. Again, some are concerned with size considerations: "I like a big dog", or "I want a small, feminine bitch".

So, it is essential to decide at the outset what you want and go for what you have decided your needs really are. If in doubt leave your options open. For instance, if you purchase a long-coated German Shepherd, then it can fulfill every purpose in working and in the role of companion-guard, but you will come nowhere at a breed show; nor should you breed with a long-coat unless you intend to 'fly in the face' of the Standard. If you want to breed or show, then you really must resist the attractions of a dog such as the long-coat!

COLOUR

White Shepherds are officially banned world-wide, though this has only been recently enforced in Great Britain, which may account for some moves to launch a club specifically for the 'White Alsatian'; which only goes to show that the white still has a following, albeit small and certainly on the 'fringe'. Other undesirable colours are: blues, pale, washed-out colours and liver-coloured. Otherwise the colour of the German Shepherd is not important, and should, from a breed standpoint, be a secondary consideration, unlike many other breeds where colour is a major factor in breeding and showing.

So, to sum up, with the above provisos, go for the colour that appeals to you — it will not be a problem. A word or two, however, should be devoted to the sable. A well-pigmented grey or golden sable is said not to be preferred by some judges. True or false, it comes back to the basic point that if the judge allows colour to overshadow other considerations, then he or she is not judging to the Standard. So if you are in doubt, find a judge who judges to the Standard!

Balance and harmony
Whatever your priorities, the puppy you choose should look balanced and 'harmonious' at seven or eight weeks, like a miniature version of the adult German Shepherd (see Chapter 8). It should not be pot-bellied or have thin bones. It should be bright eyed and energetic, and should run towards rather than away from you. Pick up the puppy; it should smell sweet and pleasant. Watch to ensure the puppy is not scratching a lot. See the puppy moving around — ideally the action should be 'true'. Ask the breeder about the mouth; if you want to show, the puppy should have a scissor bite; ask also, if it is a male puppy, about 'entirety', ie two testicles descended into the scrotum. Inspect for dew-claws:

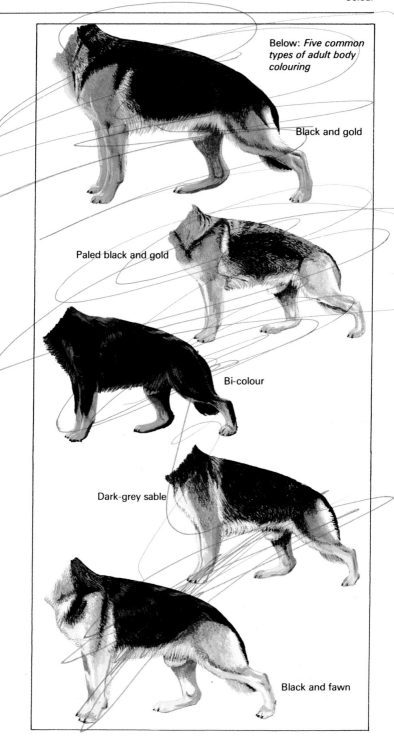

Below: *Five common types of adult body colouring*

Black and gold

Paled black and gold

Bi-colour

Dark-grey sable

Black and fawn

31

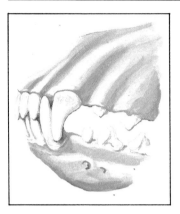

Above: *The scissor bite; where the top teeth fit over the lower ones in the front. A puppy must have this if it is to be shown.*

they should have been removed from the back legs, but not from the front legs.

The puppy you select should feel solid and firm. Do not assume, as many do, that 'big is best'. Many a small puppy has turned into a superb adult. Remember, too, that colour can change; for instance, with a black and gold, the gold will spread to even up the distribution. In all cases, be guided by the breeder who will know his or her own stock, its characteristics and development.

THE PAPERWORK

From the breeder you should expect to receive a diet sheet, the pedigree showing the ancestry of the puppy signed by the breeder, together with a registration certificate or application. Vaccinations for the 'big four': distemper, hepatitis, leptospirosis and parvovirus are normally given at 12-14 weeks. Some breeders will give the puppy injections at six weeks against distemper, using a canine distemper-measles vaccine. At the same age it is possible to give injections against parvovirus which will override the dam's immunity. This vaccine takes over the job of protecting the puppy without any dangerous gaps occurring, which can happen as soon as the mother's immunity has run out. A further inoculation may be given at nine weeks for additional protection against parvovirus.

It is necessary in those countries where rabies is endemic to consult your veterinarian in regard to vaccination, which is normally given at 12-14 weeks. You should also consult your veterinarian regarding boosters, which, so far as the 'big four' are concerned, will be administered annually. The puppy should have been wormed at least twice before seven weeks. You should ask about this, but such information is generally given on the diet sheet.

Registration

The system of registration needs explanation and will vary slightly from one country to another. What you must ensure, however, is that

and ten weeks. Tattooing in Australia is also well advanced, where, as at mid-1986, some 11,000 puppies have been tattooed. German Shepherds in Australia cannot be awarded the 'A Stamp' signifying good hips unless the dog has been tattooed. The German Shepherd Dog League of Great Britain has also approved a tattoo scheme for its members, which at the outset will be voluntary.

THE AFFIX

Until this tattoo system is fully operational, however, dog owners should be aware that a kennel club certificate of registration is the only protection available against unscrupulous breeders and dealers only in business to make fast money out of peddling 'pedigree' dogs. In some countries, such as Great Britain, it is usual for the breeder, if he or she has a Kennel Club affix, to pass over to the new owner a completed registration certificate showing the affix as the first part of the name, followed by the given name of the dog, such as: Shootersway Lido (the name including affix must not exceed 24 letters). The affix means that the kennel name is protected for the exclusive use of the breeder, when his or her dogs are named for the benefit of registration. In the United States, a kennel whose name is protected in this way is 'AKC. Reg'.

In the United States, a buyer should receive an AKC registration application form, properly filled out by the vendor. This must be completed by the new owner of the dog and submitted to the AKC with the proper fee. On the application there are spaces for first choice and second choice of names. The AKC give instructions for naming dogs, which include prohibited names. If you have purchased your puppy from a famous kennel it is possible for you to arrange with the breeder to allow you to receive the kennel name and the given name which has been selected by the breeder, though if you do this such a name cannot be changed in any way.

Above: *At five months old this dog still has one ear to lift. Ideally both your puppy's ears should be erect at six months of age.*

you have obtained genuine pedigree stock. The only way you can be certain of this is by a certificate of registration issued by the kennel club of your country. In Germany, the SV register their own stock and the purchaser of a puppy will receive an official SV pedigree certificate. Breeders' pedigrees have no role to play there. In countries outside the SV system, the breeder must register the litter with their kennel club. This cannot be done unless the parents themselves have been registered. This practice of registration in the records of the ruling body, ie the kennel club of any country, contributes much to the purity of any breed of pedigree dog. But there are those who contend that this does not go far enough; it is argued that positive identification is needed.

Consequently many countries are in the process of bringing in a tattoo system similar to that which is employed in Germany, where all German Shepherd puppies are tattooed in the ear between eight

Left: *Testing a puppy for movement and soundness. You should watch the puppy in action before you make your choice.*

Chapter Three

FEEDING AND CARE

The feeds
Herbs
Bowls and leads
Diet
Elderly dogs
Exercise

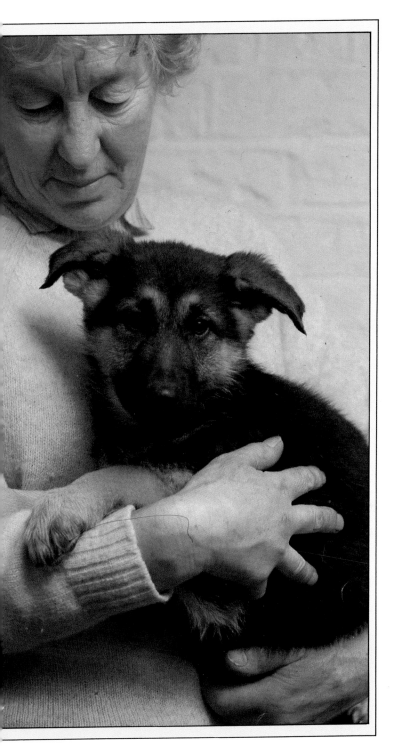

This is a very important subject and vital to the welfare and future health of your Shepherd. A lot has been written about feeding, all of which has probably succeeded to a lesser or greater degree. But before we actually go into feeding methods, it is essential to know what we are feeding for and with what. The first part of the question is easy to answer. The basis of correct feeding is to produce a dog, sound in mind and body, which will give many years of pleasure, love and devotion with the minimum of expense and anguish.

Conception

The future life and health of your Shepherd begins with conception. Both dog and bitch must be in peak condition; the dog so as to produce strong, healthy sperm; the bitch to conceive and feed the whelps within her, and once they are born to produce an adequate milk supply to rear them until weaning begins.

We will assume that a healthy litter has been born and that the bitch has been well looked after. Her puppies have been properly weaned and are ready to go to their new owners. A good breeder will give you a diet sheet and if the new puppy owner is sensible he will stick to it for at least the first few months. After this, he can change to a different method.

We are feeding to produce good bones, teeth, coat and general conformation, so we must be certain that the puppy is getting the right food, minerals and vitamins. In this way the puppy will be able to grow into a strong, healthy adult of good constitution, free from digestive problems. Correctly fed, your German Shepherd should reach a ripe old age without too many problems.

THE FEEDS

Basically, these days, there are three methods of feeding: complete feeds which can be expanded or flaked; tinned meat and biscuit meal, and finally raw meat or tripe plus biscuit meal. Dog foods are big business. New brands are springing up with unfailing regularity and the quality can be very variable. There are, however, many excellent brands in both the complete and tinned foods. How to decide which to use can be a real headache, but do take guidance from your puppy's breeder.

Availability and cost are a consideration. In some countries fresh meat and tripe are far easier

Below: *The life of your Shepherd depends a lot on the health of its parents. Here is a stud dog in excellent condition.*

and cheaper to obtain than in others but the proprietary brands of complete and tinned foods are easily obtainable throughout the world.

What is a complete feed? This is a careful blend of cereal, protein, vitamins, fats and trace elements made into a food which can come either as flakes or nuts and can be fed soaked or dry. The protein level will vary according to what is required. Growing puppies and youngsters, for example, need a far higher level of protein than an adult, while an adult who is working will need a different level to one which is a pet and which may take only daily exercise.

Complete feeds cater for dogs of all ages and from the family pet to working animals such as police dogs and guide dogs. You will find the analysis per kilogram and feeding instructions on every bag so that you will know what the dog is getting and how much it should have. There is a big difference in price between the various brands, with the expanded varieties (which refers to those feeds undergoing a certain process to ensure more complete digestion by the dog)

being the most expensive of all.

We recommend the foods using fish or meat as protein, as those using soya bean, in our experience, can lead to adverse reactions such as skin problems.

Tinned meats are expensive and we, personally, do not recommend them for a German Shepherd Dog, although many have lived long and healthy lives on this particular type of diet.

Tripe
Raw fresh meat and/or tripe plus a good quality wholemeal biscuit is still considered the best by many breeders. It is certainly the most natural diet for a carnivorous animal such as a dog and has much to recommend it. Vitamin supplements and bone meal, however, must be included to ensure healthy bones and teeth. The meat must always be very fresh and will be best kept in a deep freeze. If meat is to be cooked,

Below: *Stainless steel feeding bowls with, from the left: hard biscuits, puppy nuts, adult diet and marrow bones.*

do so very lightly as much of the goodness is lost during the cooking process.

When buying your meat, see that it is mostly lean with not too much fat on it, although a certain amount is desirable. Tripe, which is the stomach of a cow, must be fed 'green', which does not mean that the tripe is going rotten, merely that it has not been processed and made suitable for human consumption. One of the problems with tripe is the smell, which can be very unpleasant to those not used to it.

In a hot climate, it will quickly get fly-blown and needs putting into a deep freeze as soon as possible. Raw tripe is best fed in reasonable-sized pieces. Dogs love tearing at it and it is excellent for strengthening jaws and teeth.

Sheep paunches (stomachs) and heads, ox heads, udders and various other parts of the cow can all be obtained from slaughter houses and make an excellent and economical diet for your Shepherd, though they are not very practical for the owner of a single dog. If used at all it is better to obtain these already minced or cut up in small quantities for easy feeding.

In different countries, different kinds of meat are available, but if you intend to feed your Shepherd on a meat diet, make certain that it is fresh, of good quality and easily available. If you have good storage facilities, you can buy in bulk. This is more economical and you will always know that you have some readily available.

Vegetables

Raw vegetables and herbs are, these days, very much the fashion, so we must make some comments on these. The gastric juices of a dog are very strong but they cannot cope with the cellular fibres of vegetables. So, if they are fed raw vegetables, these will go straight through with very little, if any, being absorbed by the digestive system. Give your Shepherd a raw carrot to chew and you will soon see how much is digested! If raw vegetables are to be fed, they must

either be very finely grated or reduced to a pulp so as to break down the cellular fibres.

Lightly cooked and crushed vegetables are equally good but make certain that the vegetable water is included in the dog's feed otherwise half the goodness will have gone down the drain. Many dogs love fruit which can be treated in the same way as vegetables. They love eating windfall apples but take care, for too many will result in a rather dirty run to clean the next day!

HERBS

We are great believers in herbs and think that they can be very useful in controlling certain conditions. Garlic, for instance, is excellent as a general tonic and is also helpful as a worm preventative. Watercress has a high iron content, parsley and many others all have their various uses with regard to digestive disorders and skin problems. There are many excellent firms who not only supply these and many others but also sell plants for you to grow in your own garden.

When feeding fresh herbs to your Shepherd prepare them in the same way as we have advised for fresh vegetables.

Milk and eggs

Perhaps you have wondered why we have made no reference so far to milk or eggs. First, let us take milk.

All young mammals start on milk from their mothers, and in fact remain on it until such time as they are weaned on to their future adult diet.

With every species the milk formula is different, with a higher fat content, or sugar content, and so on. In our opinion, if you want healthy stock, it is totally incorrect to feed your Shepherd on anything other than bitch's milk. Cow's milk, goat's milk or any other mammal's milk is, in our opinion, totally unsuitable as a substitute.

Luckily, however, there are now several firms who make dried milk to the exact formula to that of a bitch. In the past, we have used milk for puppy-rearing, but it has always been one of these. By all means, with an older animal, the odd drink of milk will be most acceptable especially with a spoonful of honey added, though it will not be particularly beneficial health-wise.

We have never used eggs as a regular diet for either puppies or adults. If used, they are usually given to a sick adult or to a puppy in need of a light diet. The eggs are always scrambled and usually mixed with a little soaked and cooked long-grain brown rice. Rice is also useful in the diet of your elderly Shepherd, should digestive problems occur.

Chicken and fish are ideal used as a convalescent diet, but must always be cooked and the bones removed.

THE NEW PUPPY

The day has arrived for you to collect your puppy. Prior to picking it up, you will have given thought to its welfare once it arrives with you. Where is it going to live — inside or out? What sort of bedding will it require? A collar, lead, feeding and water bowls plus grooming gear will also have to be bought.

You will have discussed diet with the breeder and made suitable arrangements for obtaining and storing the food you will need. If the puppy is to be kept inside, find somewhere where it can be on its

Below: *The arrival of your new puppy is a pleasure, but careful thought should always be given to its future welfare.*

own. A conservatory is ideal or even use the space under the kitchen table. You can get excellent plastic baskets, which are strong and also easy to keep clean; a blanket inside will make this an ideal place for your puppy to sleep.

It is an advantage if the floor of the room you have chosen is washable as accidents can occur with a very young puppy (see also training, Chapter 4). If possible, have an outside run and kennel available. This will always be useful to put the puppy in if you have visitors, or, if you have bought a bitch, when she is in season. Choose a site close to the house with good drainage facilities (for easy cleaning). The kennel should be brick built with a double roof for both heat and cold protection. Site the kennel with its back to the prevailing wind. The size we advise is 2m x 3m (6ft x 9ft) with a height of 2m (6ft) sloping to 1.5m (4½ft).

Have a door on one side, metal lined, and of a height that you can easily use. Include a window of unbreakable glass or Perspex which can be opened, lined inside with welded mesh. If the puppy is to live outside, it is advisable to have cavity walls and do not forget the damp-course. Concrete floors for both run and kennels are the best.

When building your kennel, make certain it is damp-proof and draught-proof. A German Shepherd Dog can put up with intense cold but draughts and damp are fatal to its well-being. Onto this add a reasonable-sized run — up to 3m x 4m (9ft x 12ft) — preferably covered, with a gate at one end and fenced with 2m (6ft) high chain-link or welded mesh (better still but more expensive). Inside the kennel make a bed out of wood, 1m x 2m (3ft x 6ft), which gives the dog ample room to stretch out, with sides 0.5m (1½ft) high. By adding higher sides this can double up as a whelping bed if, at a later stage, you decide to try your hand at breeding. Add a blanket or Vetbed to lie on. We use wood shavings, which we feel are preferable to straw, around the

outside of the bed, so that if the dog has to relieve itself during the night it can do so and everything will be absorbed. Other bedding materials such as foam rubber mattresses with removable covers, bean bags, etc make lovely beds but are best left until after your puppy has finished his chewing stage!

Wooden kennels
We do not advise wooden kennels because, although initially cheaper, they need a lot of upkeep. A bored dog loves sharpening its teeth on them. They are excessively cold in winter and can get very hot in summer. Country and climate must be carefully considered when building your kennel.

Do not forget to give some thought to the disposal of faeces and old bedding. If you are using wood shavings then this can be burnt, preferably in an incinerator; it may be taken away to a dump; or, if you are a keen gardener, it will make excellent compost.

BOWLS AND LEADS

We always use stainless steel water and feeding bowls. They are easy to keep clean and will last for years. We do not favour plastic bowls; they are difficult to keep clean especially if your puppy has sharpened its teeth on them, which is all too often! Earthenware bowls can be broken, so use stainless steel which are by far the best in the long run.

If you intend your dog to wear a collar, get a stout, adjustable, good quality leather one and it will last a lifetime. On it can be put the dog's name, your name, address and telephone number by means of identification should the dog get lost. This should never happen with a well looked after and trained Shepherd but, of course, the odd accident can always occur! You want a good quality leather lead — not too thick or thin — about 2m (6ft) long, preferably hand sewn or plaited, with a bayonet-type clip. This sort of lead is ideal for

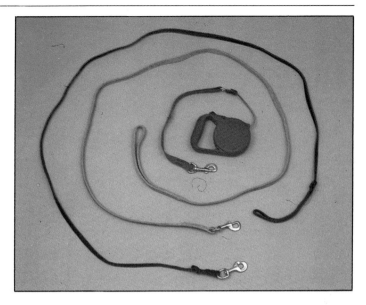

Above: *A selection of leads suitable for a German Shepherd, with a Flexi-lead in the centre. Notice the bayonet-type clips.*

---

training purposes as well as for everyday use.

For early lead training, we recommend a nylon or leather slip collar which is kind on your puppy but which can later be replaced by a check chain. We favour the long-linked light chain collars; an adult GSD requires one 61cm (24in) in length. The long-linked check chains are less harsh and will not cut the coat as the fine ones will. Nothing is so unbecoming as to see a Shepherd with all the hair cut on one side of its neck. And please, no chain leads. Just imagine the state of your hand when, and if, your GSD starts pulling! A nylon lead will do the same so avoid both these types and stick to leather.

Below: *An essential grooming kit should include: chamois leather, metal comb, wire brush and a polishing pad.*

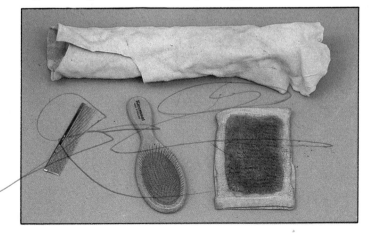

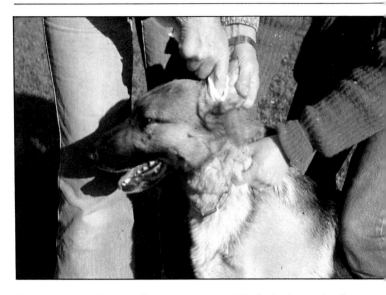

Above: *Your regular grooming routine should always include a careful inspection and cleaning of your dog's ears.*

Below: *Nail clipping is occasionally necessary, but must be done with a great deal of care to avoid cutting the quick.*

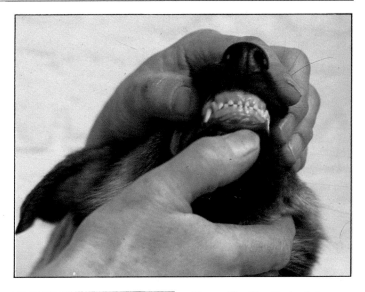

COAT CARE

Your Shepherd, because of its weather resisting coat, is not difficult to keep clean. If it gets wet, a good shake and it is practically dry. All the grooming equipment necessary is a metal comb, wire brush and a dusteror chamois leather. Get your puppy used to its grooming routine right from the start. Begin with a quick brush, then check the ears and mouth, all very gently. Praise when you have finished. Gradually extend this routine by using the comb and also picking up and checking the feet. Make it a happy experience, so if at any time your puppy has to have mouth, ears or teeth looked at, it will be quite used to it.

A Shepherd will lose its coat twice a year and it is at these times that grooming is of extra importance. With the GSD's double coat (wool undercoat, hard topcoat) a lot comes out, but once the new coat is through it will need a minimum of attention to keep it in shining condition. Do not be surprised if your Shepherd loses weight when coating; it is quite natural and nothing to worry about, its condition will be back to normal when the new coat comes through.

Above: *Checking the teeth for tartar. Examining your puppy is always easier if you have begun the routine at an early age.*

DIET

The breeder will give you a diet sheet, so you will know what type of feed you should use. We now use a complete diet which we have found most successful in producing good bones, growth and condition with little or no digestive problems. It is easy to store but must be kept in a dry, vermin-proof place. This, however, should prove no difficulty for the owner of a single dog as he will probably only be buying one 20kg (44lb) sack at a time. If, however, you find that some has become mouldy, discard at once as it will be detrimental to your puppy's health. The complete feed we favour has a content of 30% protein and 11.5% fat, together with all the vitamins, calcium and trace elements in the correct ratio, so that nothing extra need be added. It is most important, in fact, that nothing extra, especially in the form of vitamins, should be added as this could upset the carefully produced balance, resulting in bone problems such as rickets.

Puppy feed

When your puppy arrives it will be seven to eight weeks old. At this stage it should be having 80-110g (3-4oz) of feed — weighed dry then soaked in hot water — four times daily. For the first few days it might go off its food and its motions might be a little loose. This will be due to a change of environment, losing all its puppy friends and the general upheaval.

A puppy with a stable temperament will soon get over this and be back to normal in next to no time. Give it plenty of toys, such as an old shoe, a ball (provided this is made of hard rubber and too large to swallow), and a squeaky toy. All of these will help make your new puppy more content.

Gradually increase the size of the meals but start cutting down the number at around 14-16 weeks. At six months it will be eating ½-¾ kg (1-1¾ lb) divided into two meals a day. If it is to live outside, get your puppy used to being in its run by feeding it there. Whether in the house or outside, always have plenty of clean, fresh drinking water available.

Below: *A 12-year-old Shepherd in excellent condition. Special care should be taken with the diet and exercise of elderly dogs.*

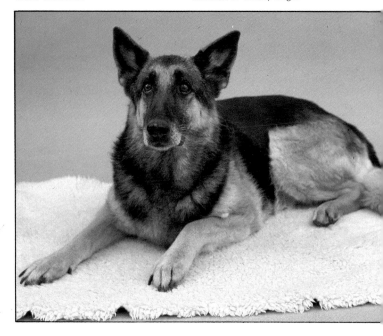

Fat puppy
We like our puppies to be well-covered but not excessively fat. A rough guide is that you should be able to feel the ribs but not see them. If your puppy looks too thin, first check for worms. If it is clear, then increase the food intake. It is better that the puppy should be too thin than too fat, as excessive weight can do a lot of harm to soft bones. One must always remember that these are not fully calcified until about 12 months of age, so that carrying excessive weight could damage them.

At 12 months of age your Shepherd will start the adult diet on which it will remain for the rest of its life. This is still a complete diet, but one with only 20% protein. We sometimes add raw meat and tripe to this for taste and variety.

The adults will get about ¾-1kg (1¾-2lb) daily, depending on the time of year. If your dog lives entirely outside and you live in a cold climate, then its food intake should be increased. From an early age, a marrow bone should be given once a week.

Above: *Puppies of three months feeding together. From 14-16 weeks their meals will be increased in size but reduced in number.*

Elderly dogs
We have 12- and 13-year-old Shepherds who have remained fit and healthy throughout their lives fed on the diet detailed above. If, however, in old age your Shepherd develops kidney problems or gets too fat then possibly a diet change is indicated. In such cases it is best to consult your vet. Sometimes an elderly dog is better fed two or three small feeds daily rather than one big one, and as an elderly dog takes less exercise, less food should be required.

One wheat-germ capsule and one capsule of seaweed preparation added to the diet, we find excellent in relieving rheumatic aches and pains. Check regularly for any lumps or bumps and if you have a bitch make certain there are none on her milk glands. If any are found then you are advised to consult your vet immediately.

EXERCISE

We cannot finish this chapter without some mention of exercise, which plays such an important part in your Shepherd's welfare. As puppies, running around your garden is quite sufficient. Get your puppy used to the lead so that when all inoculations are complete (these should be finished by 14 weeks) you are able to take it for short walks outside so as to get it used to traffic and unfamiliar people and sounds.

Puppy lead training can begin as soon as your puppy has settled in. Start with a nylon check collar. Attach your lead and let the puppy run about like this for a few minutes. Then take hold of the lead but let the puppy take you where it wants.

The next stage is to encourage it to come to you by using its favourite toy and gentle pressure on the lead. On first feeling the pull on its neck it will probably act against it. Release the pressure immediately, go and comfort it.

Above: Early lead training helped by encouraging the puppy with its favourite toy. Keep the training enjoyable for your puppy.

Below: The puppy's first lesson on the lead and check collar. Its fears can be overcome with patience and regular training.

Repeat the exercise, then take off the check collar and have a good game. Repeat this daily and within a few days your puppy will be happy on the lead.

Only short distances should be covered to start with, and busy main streets with their crowds and huge lorries should be avoided. Build up to this gradually so that at six months your dog is happy in reasonable traffic. You can also start taking it for walks in your local park or, if in the country, in the fields. Do not, though, take it off the lead until it will come immediately when called.

Gradually increase the amount of exercise until you are spending an hour a day, consisting of road work and free-range running, which is what your Shepherd requires at 12 months. We do not believe a Shepherd needs ten miles or more daily, but it must have one good walk and then be let out morning and last thing at night in order to relieve itself. If, however, the Shepherd is required for Working Trials, it must be kept fit.

Feeding and Care Check List

If your puppy or adult refuses a meal, take the food away and try again at the next mealtime

If your Shepherd is sick or has diarrhoea but is its usual self, starve it for two days on water only and then return it gradually to its usual diet

If the condition persists and your Shepherd becomes listless and generally off-colour then visit the vet

Avoid giving titbits to Shepherds of any age and never feed at table. This can become a nuisance

Your puppy will have been wormed two or three times before leaving the breeder. After this it is advisable to worm every six to eight weeks until your puppy is twelve months, then worm once a year

In America worming is done to protect against a wide variety of parasites, so make certain you use a preparation which deals with them all

In very hot climates your Shepherd will have to be dipped every week against parasites such as ticks and fleas. In all climates care should be taken with external parasites

Inoculations vary from one country to another; one of the most important being rabies. Check with your local vet as to what is required in your particular area. Rabies inoculations are not required in Britain

Inoculations are very important and some need boosting every six months, others every twelve months. Always make certain that your Shepherd is up to date. Let your motto be: "Better safe than sorry"

Chapter Four

TRAINING YOUR GERMAN SHEPHERD

House training
Socialisation
Sit and heel work
Sit stay
Recall
Finish
Retrieve

TRAINING

Unless you are prepared to give time every day to training, do not buy a GSD or, for that matter, any other dog. Like children, dogs need discipline, and without this can become a source of constant worry. A well-trained dog, on the other hand, is a joy to own and something one can feel justifiably proud of.

Before your puppy arrives, give careful thought to the name. Choose a name of one or two syllables which has plenty of punch to it, for both correction and praise. Think carefully about the tone of your voice when addressing your dog; make it firm for correction, higher and happier for praise. Decide on what words of command you will use and always stick to them. Keep to simple words such as 'come', 'sit', 'down', 'stay', 'no' and 'find'.

ATTITUDE

A great deal has been written about training but we believe that seldom is anything mentioned about the dog's attitude towards it. So put yourself in your puppy's position and see training from a dog's point of view.

A puppy lives by instinct, which is the will to survive. Basically this means finding food, warmth, comfort and, most importantly, a pack leader. This *must* be you. Up until it arrives with you, first its mother, then after weaning, the breeder, has taken on this role. Now it is your turn. Your puppy has come to new surroundings, new smells, new faces and most important, *no* litter mates. It is on its own in a strange world. So, decide on a routine for feeding, playtime, training, sleeping and stick to it. You are channelling its instincts which we call 'fixing'. If adhered to, this process will be of great benefit when more serious training commences.

Noise

You have put your puppy to bed, in a place of your choice, and it starts crying. Do not go down to comfort it. If you do, it will soon realise that by crying it can get comfort and you have put the first nail in your coffin as a pack leader.

On the other hand, do not attempt to stop the crying by shouting at it; the puppy will not have a clue what you mean and

Below: *Making friends is a very important step in your German Shepherd's development from puppy to fully socialised adult.*

you will have simply started a chain of doubts in its mind. Just endure it and in the morning give lots of praise, take it outside for toilet purposes and have a game, even though you may well be desperately suffering from a lack of sleep! After a night or two the puppy will soon stop crying; this is not intelligence but instinct. You have successfully started your 'fixing' programme. If, however, you have neighbour problems, a hot bottle wrapped in a towel put in the puppy's bed will help and, if all else fails, a mild sedative, but discontinue this as soon as possible.

HOUSE TRAINING

Base your house training on the same principle. When does your puppy want to relieve itself? This is usually on waking, after feeding and during play. Knowing this, decide where in the garden its toilet area is to be and always take the puppy there. We stress the point on 'taking' it out rather than just 'putting' it out. This is most important.

If you put the puppy outside the door and leave it, all it will do is sit there and cry. What has it done wrong? Another seed of doubt is sown in its poor little mind. So, whatever the weather, stay with it, ignoring all overtures to play until

the job has been done. Then praise it and indulge in some games. The 'fixing' process has taken another step in the right direction.

Never chastise a puppy if it goes in the wrong place unless you actually catch it in the act — then give it a firm 'no' and take the puppy outside. It is advisable, if the puppy is in the house, to put some newspaper down near the door during the night as accidents can easily happen with a very young puppy.

By following this routine you will soon have a house-trained puppy.

Chewing

Chewing can sometimes be a problem especially between the ages of four and six months when the puppy is teething. Make sure that it has plenty of sensible toys (see Chapter 3) and do not leave anything of a chewable nature around for it to get hold of. Remember, we are talking about dealing with instinct, and not intelligence. This means if punishment is given for what happened an hour ago, the puppy will have no idea why it is being

Below: *It is most important that your Shepherd should learn to mix happily with dogs and other types of animals.*

reprimanded, and so the doubts as to how it should behave will continue to grow. Follow the rules suggested, above, on the other hand and your puppy will be learning by the association of ideas. The 'fixing' process will be well underway and you will have made the first important step in becoming pack leader.

SOCIALISATION

Socialisation is continually in progress, your puppy is learning to live with you, adapting itself to various noises such as the washing machine, vacuum, television and the general sounds associated with the house. Let it find its own level in doing this; do not force it into any situation. Give plenty of praise though when it begins to investigate of its own accord. This is all part of character training and a most important part of the puppy's education.

Below: *Socialisation should be a continual process for your puppy, but let it take its own time to discover new sights and sounds.*

Car travel

As car travel is so important nowadays, get your puppy used to it as quickly as possible. Begin by sitting it in the car for short periods every day, first of all with you and then on its own. Then take it for short rides so that it enjoys its time in the car, knowing that it will always be coming back home again.

Basic drives

With the next stage of training, we must consider the puppy's basic drives. These are pursuit, social and defence; or in other words the chasing, friendliness and guarding instincts. To control pursuit and defence, we must first cultivate a will to please which in turn will lead to a happy worker. Make certain you have a daily playtime.

Let your puppy tug at a piece of rag or chase a ball. Find out what toy it really likes and use this as part of your praise when an exercise is correctly done. Sit on the ground and let it jump on you; have a really good rough and tumble, you are now taking the place of its litter mates. Throw its favourite toy one or two metres

away from you so that its natural instinct is to bring the article back to you. Give it plenty of praise, both verbal and touch. As soon as its concentration starts to wane, and this will happen very quickly with a young puppy, stop.

This play routine is most important as it constitutes part of the praise routine. If the puppy tries to bite or gets too excited, calm everything down. The pursuit drive is controlled with recall training, the social drive should be developing in everyday procedures and the defence drive is something which is desirable but must not be allowed to get out of control.

Food instinct

When feeding your puppy, make it sit for its food by holding the bowl well above its head while giving the command of 'sit'. It will probably jump up to start with but then will sit. As soon as this happens, praise it and immediately put down the bowl of food. The puppy will soon get the idea. Now try a recall. Get a friend to hold the puppy, then walk

Above: *Most German Shepherd Dogs enjoy car travel, but it is important that you get your puppy used to being in a car.*

Above: *Play articles such as a fun rag, rubber toys and small wooden dumb-bell are invaluable aids to early training.*

away with the food bowl, rattling it to get the puppy's attention. Put the bowl down in front of you and as you give the command of the puppy's name and 'come', have the puppy released. In these two exercises you are training it by appealing to its basic instinct: food.

Above: *The correct way to put on a check chain. Looped in this way the moment the dog ceases to pull, the chain will go loose.*

CHECK CHAINS

Early lead training has been dealt with in the previous chapter and you have begun to use a long-linked check chain. This must be put on correctly. The lead is attached to the ring of the check chain going over the top of the neck. This will ensure that as soon as the pressure is released on the lead the chain will go loose. Always work your dog on the left hand side.

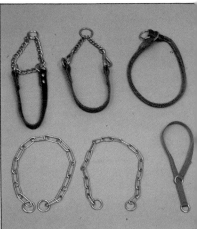

Above right: *Check collars.* **Top:** *Two collars for showing and a leather collar.* **Bottom:** *Check chains and a nylon check collar.*

Right: *Teaching 'Lido' to sit. Notice particularly the positions and correct use of the right and left hands in this exercise.*

SIT AND HEEL WORK

Serious heel work can also now begin. At the moment your puppy knows the command of 'sit', but so far in your exercises it has always sat in front of you with the incentive of food to keep its attention. Now it has got to realise that 'sit' can also mean sitting at your side without the promise of food as a reward. This can be a little muddling at first, and cause some confusion, so the best way to avoid this is to gently enforce the command in the following way:

First bring the puppy round to your left hand side; say its name and a firm command of 'sit'

At the same time give an upward jerk with the lead (held in the right hand), while with the left you firmly push down on its croup

Your puppy is now sitting at your left hand side and so is now ready to begin to learn how to accomplish heel work:

Above: *The Sit. This is the position from which the Recall and Retrieve, several advanced exercises and heel work all begin.*

Say the dog's name and the command 'heel'

Step forward with your left foot and at the same time give a sharp jerk on the check chain

The puppy will come with you

It will probably bound forward, so stand still and when it has got to the end of the lead, do an about turn giving the firm command of 'heel'

When it is back with you, praise and continue walking. Do the same again if it bounds forward.

Walk two or three times up and down the garden, always finishing with a sit. You will find the puppy's attention going at this stage, so let it off the lead and start a game.

To get your puppy concentrating for heel work try having its favourite play article in your left hand. It will look up at you and as you move forward it will follow you and the toy. Continue in this way for a few minutes every day and you will soon find your puppy is

doing good heel work. When it is proficient you can begin to include left and right turns as well as about-turns.

When your puppy is working well with this, without the use of lead or left hand, then the time has come to start off-lead heel work. If at any time the puppy deviates from your side, then go back on the lead.

Keep your sessions short and happy, and always finish with a play routine. Heel work can get awfully boring if it is kept up too long, and this is often the cause of lagging and sluggish heel work.

Left: *'Tiber' responding successfully to his play article during the early stages of heel work training.*

Right: *The heel work exercise begins with the dog in the sit position. Notice that the dog is positioned on the left hand side of the handler.*

Below: *With the dog's close attention, heel work commences. Note that the handler's left leg takes the first step.*

Below: *Accomplishing good heel work. Your training sessions should be short but frequent and always finish with a game.*

SIT STAY

We are now ready to start the 'sit' and 'down' stays. Your puppy already knows what 'sit' means, so we will start with this. In all previous exercises we have used the dog's name first and then a command. The 'stay' exercises are static, so do not use the name, simply give the firm command of 'sit stay'.

Get your dog sitting on your left side

With your left hand in front of the dog's nose, give a firm command of 'sit stay'. Move to the front, still holding the lead in the right hand in a position where if the dog tries to move to you, you can give a jerk backwards, repeating the command 'stay'

After a few seconds return to its side

Give a release command and take a step backwards. We use the release command of 'OK', but anything similar is equally good. The backward step is to prevent any confusion in the puppy's mind with the heel exercise

After the release give plenty of praise

Repeat two or three times

When your puppy is steady on this, try walking round behind its back, still keeping the lead taut in case it tries to move. Gradually progress by moving two or three paces away from its side and front, releasing the lead pressure at the same time. The left hand in front of the nose comes in very useful when moving away. Gradually increase the distance. Then put the lead on the ground, and finally discard it altogether.

Never progress to the next stage until your puppy is absolutely

Above: *The beginning of the Sit and Stay exercise. In this routine only the command is used and not the dog's name.*

steady on the last. If the puppy at any time breaks its stay, you know you have failed to consolidate, so you must go back to the beginning. The 'stay' is not a difficult exercise to teach provided you don't rush things, but once the puppy gets in the habit of breaking a stay it is very difficult to correct — so be warned! Do not try to do too much in any one session; it is much better to concentrate on one exercise in the morning and another in the afternoon.

Play

We cannot stress enough the importance of ending your training with a play routine. If, right from the start, your puppy thoroughly enjoys its play and its fun articles, it will soon realise that working correctly means a fun period to come. This association of ideas is of the utmost importance.

If you always insist on immediate obedience before the fun routine you are well on your way to becoming the pack leader.

Top: *Walking away from your dog during the Sit and Stay. This degree of control can only come after work and practice.*

Above: *Giving the command 'stay'. Notice the handler's use of her left hand to enforce the command in front of the dog.*

DOWN STAY

We must now teach the command of 'down'. We find we get less resistance from the dog by first teaching this from the sit position, so begin the routine by sitting your Shepherd by your side.

Using your left hand, push the dog's shoulder away from you and at the same time give a downward jerk with the lead. Give the command 'down stay' firmly

You will have caught your Shepherd off balance and it will have gone down. But be sure that you get down by its side, stroking its head to give it confidence and thus avoiding a struggle

In a soothing voice repeat 'down stay' for a few seconds and then give the release command. Let the dog jump up and give plenty of praise

Now continue as for the 'sit stay'

When your dog is going down on command from the sit position without any help from you, try the same from a standing position.

Above: *The early training of the Down command. Note the positions of the handler's hands as she teaches the movement.*

In the meantime, you will have been taking your puppy out for walks along busy roads and to places where it can run free. Always make it sit at the kerb before crossing, and make sure that it is not pulling when walking on the lead.

When your puppy is running free always have a long lead attached to it so that it cannot get away from you.

Free ranging
Your dog will know the meaning of the word 'come' by now, so when it is free ranging give the command occasionally. If your Shepherd does not come immediately, get hold of the long line and give it a hard jerk. When it begins to return to you, give plenty of praise and on reaching you reward it with a titbit.

Do this several times when out walking so that your puppy knows that it must return to you immediately on the command 'come'.

Likewise, as your puppy is becoming more proficient on its 'down', give it the command when it is two or three metres away from you. If it does not react immediately you still need to consolidate on ground work, when you are in a position to enforce your command.

Work hard on the instant 'down', away from you, as this can be invaluable if your puppy starts to chase something. If you can drop it on one command you know you are safe in case of an emergency.

Hide and seek
When out walking use your ingenuity to find interesting things for your puppy to do. For instance, throw one of its favourite toys into the long grass and encourage it to 'find'. If out with a friend, get him to hold your puppy whilst you go and hide. Puppies and adults love finding their owners and in this fun game you are teaching it elementary tracking. Any small ditches or tree trunks can be used

to encourage your puppy to clamber over — a prelude to jumping which most Shepherds love. Do not under any circumstances let it jump anything over 30-40cm (12-16in) high until it is over 12 months of age or you will do untold damage to young and still soft bones.

Get your puppy used to being tied up. Use a leather collar, tie it up for short periods, then gradually increase the length of time. Once your puppy realises that you will return, it will stay tied contentedly for as long as you wish. *Never* use a check chain for this because strangulation can happen all too easily.

RECALL

The next stage is to put the commands of 'sit' and 'come' together in one sequence which will flow together.

Below: *The first stage in teaching the Recall. The dog must sit on the lead and wait patiently for the command to 'come'.*

With its lead on, stand in front facing your dog and give a firm command of 'sit'

Still holding the lead, take two or three steps backwards and at the same time give the command 'come', together with a smart jerk on the lead

Continue moving backwards while using the lead to bring the dog up to you

Halt, use a smart command of 'sit', and the dog will be sitting straight in front of you

Return to its side, give the release command and lots of praise

Begin the routine again

When this is perfected, giving a firm command of 'sit', move back to the end of the lead and call the dog in without moving backwards. Then take the lead off and make the dog sit for longer intervals before calling it.

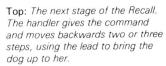

Top: *The next stage of the Recall. The handler gives the command and moves backwards two or three steps, using the lead to bring the dog up to her.*

Above: *A straight sit in front. With the dog in front of her, the handler has given the command 'sit', to complete the Recall. Notice the dog's complete attention to the handler.*

Above right: *Practising the Finish, an essential exercise for Competitive Obedience or Working Trials. Being accomplished is a left hand finish with the dog pivoting on its front legs.*

The next step is to increase the distance you are away from it. On no account let your dog come to you before you give the command. Sometimes return to it without calling it so that your GSD gets the idea that it must only come when you call.

When it is absolutely steady on this, then go and stand by its side. Give a firm command of 'sit' using your left hand to enforce it. Step off with your right foot. Your dog associates the left foot moving forward with heel work; this time, however, you do not want it to come with you. Walk out several metres, turn and halt. Call your dog.

FINISH

Now let us concentrate our attention on the Finish. This is a formal exercise which for the owner of a pet dog is not strictly necessary.

It is, however, a worthwhile routine to master for the sake of discipline, and if you have any ambitions to work in Competitive Obedience or Working Trials it is essential knowledge.

The Finish is used after the formal Recall and Retrieve exercise and consists of bringing the dog to heel at your left side from the sit position in front of you. There are two ways of going about this — the right hand and the left hand finish. We will explain the method of the right hand finish first.

Tell your dog to 'sit', and stand in front of it

Take the lead in your right hand, with not too much slack

Give the command of 'heel' and give the lead a firm jerk, at the same time moving the right arm back in line with the right leg which takes one step back

Keeping the lead tight, guide your dog into a position slightly behind the right leg. Transfer the lead from right to left hand, at the same time replace your right leg to its original position

Your dog has now been guided to the 'sit' position

Give the command 'sit'. If the dog does not sit immediately on this command, then quickly transfer the lead back to your right hand so that the left hand remains free to enforce the command.

Right: *The first stage in teaching the Retrieve. The handler teaches the dog to hold a wooden dumb-bell securely.*

The left hand finish is accomplished in a similar fashion by taking a pace back with the left foot

The lead is still held in the right hand, but use the left hand, holding the lead close to the check chain, to make an anti-clockwise circling motion, thus guiding the dog into the heel position

At the same time bring the left foot back to its original position

In the left hand finish, the dog does not go behind you but swivels round on its front legs to finish sitting beside you

Until your Shepherd is perfect on the recall, practice the Finish at a different time or you will find it will start anticipating and go straight to heel without sitting in front of you.

RETRIEVE

By now your puppy through its play routine can retrieve various articles including metal, and is happy to pick these up and bring them back to you. But so far it has done so only when it wants to.

Your first step must therefore be to teach it the command 'hold'. This requires a dumb-bell. We favour a light, square ended type

With both you and your Shepherd facing the same direction, make it sit in between your legs

Now gently caress its throat with your left hand so that it is looking up at you

With the dumb-bell in your right hand, gently press it against the puppy's front teeth, giving the command 'hold'

Usually the dog will open its mouth so you can slip the dumb-bell in

If you meet with resistance, use the finger and thumb of your free hand to press on either side of the bottom jaw, and the mouth will open

With the dumb-bell in the mouth, and with you still holding it, continue gently stroking the puppy's throat and give the command 'hold'

Then say the command 'give' and take the dumb-bell out of its mouth

Give lots of praise

Whatever happens, do not let it drop the dumb-bell before you have given the command of 'give'. If it does, go back to the beginning again. It is only after this work is accomplished perfectly that you can start throwing the dumb-bell, and then only a short distance.

Sit the dog at your side, then put a finger through the check chain around its neck so that it cannot move away from you until commanded to do so

You have perfected your recall and your 'hold' so your Shepherd should go out, pick up the dumb-bell with no mouthing, return to the sit in front of you, holding the dumb-bell until you say 'give'

As with all the other exercises always make certain that the dog knows what it should be doing and that it is doing it well before taking the next step. Having perfected these exercises, you will have succeeded in training a German Shepherd you can take anywhere knowing that it is always under perfect control.

It is inadvisable to start this exercise until after six months of age, when teething has been completed. Whatever you do, do not hurt your dog's mouth. When your puppy is taking hold of the dumb-bell on its own, then repeat the exercise with you standing in front. Hold the dumb-bell in front of its nose and make the puppy have to reach out for it.

When this exercise is happily achieved, put the dumb-bell on the ground and encourage your dog to pick it up. Finally tell it to 'sit', walk out a few paces and put the dumb-bell on the ground. Go back to your dog's side, give it the command of 'hold' and off it will go.

As soon as the dumb-bell is picked up, call the dog back to you. If it does not return immediately, put it on to the long line or lead and repeat the exercise.

Top right: *Having made the retrieve, the dog makes a smart return to the handler with the dumb-bell still held secure.*

Below: *The Shepherd when commanded goes straight out for the pick-up. This should be done neatly with no mouthing.*

Below: *The dog returns immediately to the sit position in front of the handler with the dumb-bell still held.*

Bottom: *Only at the command 'give' should the dog release the dumb-bell to the handler. The dumb-bell must not be dropped.*

ESSENCE OF TRAINING

Consistency of training is the essence of a well-trained Shepherd. A little every day is far better than a lot one day and then nothing for a week. Always make certain your dog knows what you mean before either chastising it or going on to the next stage. If, at any time, your dog does not obey, you must think back to where you went wrong and then start the exercise again from there. Do not go on to another exercise until the one you are doing is really 'fixed'. Ideally you should practice one exercise in the morning and another in the afternoon.

You can do much inside the house, such as elementary recall, sit, retrieve and stays. Make it do an exercise before it gets fed. At a later stage, you can replace the food with titbits and then cut them out too. Your fun routine is most important for this is the reward for correctly executed work, but food can be useful to start with.

Walks

Before going for a walk make your puppy sit while you put on its check chain and lead. Incorporate your fun routine while out on walks. By the time it is six months old it should be doing heel work on-lead, sit and down stays off-lead with you standing about three metres away, and a reasonable distance recall off-lead.

Training club

It is now time to take your puppy to your local training club for socialising with other dogs and people. If it shows any signs of aggression towards the dogs, give the command of 'no' with a sharp jerk on the check chain. If this does not work, hold it with one hand on either side of its head and give it a really good shaking, repeating the command 'no'. Do not be surprised if it does not work particularly well the first time there. Be patient because there is much to divert your puppy's attention because everything will be very new and strange.

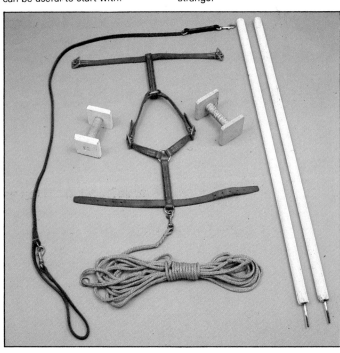

CONCLUSION

The training we have suggested in this chapter is ideal for the well-reared Shepherd of good character. If you have one which is very nervous, aggressive or constantly ailing, obviously the whole routine might have to be modified. If you have a problem dog we suggest that you seek professional help, as it is impossible to deal with the subject in a book of this size.

If you have enjoyed training your Shepherd to this standard and have the inclination to go further, you will find that in these exercises we have given you a sound foundation. The way is now clear to start tracking, searching, agility (when old enough), and the other exercises your Shepherd is so capable of doing. You have proved yourself as the undisputed pack leader and your Shepherd will now give you its complete loyalty, love and respect.

Left: *Equipment for advanced training exercises, including training lead, tracking harness, tracking poles and dumb-bells.*

Above: *A German Shepherd on a tracking exercise in lead and harness. Notice the amount of distance from the handler.*

Below: *Advanced exercises of the type used to train guide dogs for the blind. Here a GSD is being taught to avoid hazards.*

Below: *A Working Trials exercise. This is the 2m (6ft) scale. Other trials include the 1m (3ft) clear jump and 3m (9ft) long jump*

Chapter Five

STARTING A KENNEL

The building
Bedding
Importing

We have often been asked: how did you start your kennel of German Shepherds?

To begin with you must have genuine interest in the breed. A modicum of talent certainly helps and a background of animal husbandry, say in farming, is invaluable. You should also possess that indescribable 'feel' for animals. In running a kennel you *must* be able to establish an essential rapport with a number of different dogs, so that by their particular characteristics and behavioural patterns they all become individuals to you. Finally, you must have a clear understanding of the breed standard and its traditions, and the willingness to be true at all costs to the ideals of the world German Shepherd community.

One of your first considerations should be to decide exactly what kind of kennel you want to set up; you will need to make up your mind so that you can choose what kind of property and land will best suit you. Are you interested in training as well as breeding the German Shepherd? Do you want to compete in obedience and working trials? Do you intend to exhibit your Shepherds in the show ring? You may, of course, already be doing some of these things with dogs you already own.

THE LOCATION

Ideally you should select a country location not too far from a city or town. Always remember that suppliers and visitors need to be able to reach you easily. Keep neighbours as far away as possible, not because you are anti-social but because, with the noise of the dogs, you will not want to give cause for complaint.

Make sure that you have plenty of access and parking space. On a busy day with puppies to sell or visits from other GSD enthusiasts, you might need plenty of space for vehicles.

The choice of dwelling and the size of the land will depend, naturally, on your personal and family requirements and the amount you wish to spend; though you will need enough land for kennels and runs, and for a training area as well.

Once you have decided exactly what you need, you will find that from time to time kennel properties come up for sale; amongst these you may find exactly what you are looking for at the price you are prepared to pay.

KENNEL CONSTRUCTION AND LAYOUT

In describing the kennel layout, we will only be dealing with basic kennel designs as we do not profess architectural or building skills. It will obviously be necessary to consult construction experts to work out detailed plans, but even when viewing pre-designed and, indeed, ready-made structures, it is as well to go in with a good idea of how you want your kennels to look. You should also bear in mind that any building plans may be subject to the approval of the appropriate local or state authority.

Fencing
The first thing to look at is the fencing of the land. The best material is substantial chain-link or welded mesh, secured by concrete posts. The fence should be at least 2m (6ft) high. Choose posts where the top 30cm (1ft) is angled inwards as this will make it difficult for the dogs to scale the fence.

Avoid using plastic-covered chain-link, as the metal inside, in our experience, will not stand up to the hard wear a Shepherd might give it. The plastic covering is designed to prevent rust, but strength is more important, and galvanised-metal link will give adequate rust protection.

Strong gates can be hung on the concrete posts, the gates themselves constructed of a frame of angle-iron or tubular-steel, 'filled in' with chain-link or welded mesh.

Grouping
The principle to follow in regard to

the kennel buildings and runs is that of convenient grouping. As much as possible should be situated for the minimum amount of labour and effort. Remember your kennel will be a working environment.

We recommend brick or concrete construction for the kennels themselves. Wooden window casements and doors may be incorporated, but they should be covered with sheet-metal, otherwise your doors and window frames will become fair game for the jaws of your Shepherds. If you are considering a block of, say, ten kennels to house a maximum of 20 dogs, with adjacent runs, try to ensure that the runs are facing away from the worst aspects of the prevailing weather; cold winds or tropical sun, whichever is your particular problem.

THE BUILDING

In choosing a kennel, it is as well to know about the relative merits of the classic brick or concrete-block type of construction as against the more modern type of pre-cast, modular kennel unit.

Above: *The gate into the run should open both inwards and outwards for convenience. Sliding metal bolts allow for locking.*

The latter usually comes in a standard height or depth, say of 2m (6ft) and 1.5m (4½ft) respectively. Often a choice of width inside the kennel is offered, either 1.5m (4½ft), 2m (6ft) or 2.5m (7½ft). These unit measurements depend, of course, on the manufacturer concerned, but probably won't vary to any great extent.

The units are generally made of concrete slabs, the inside of which should be smooth for easy cleaning. The units are rigidly secured with brackets, nuts and bolts, which should all be galvanised to resist rust. The roof will also consist of concrete slab units which may be covered with roofing felt. The complete kennel may be set on a concrete base. The enclosures for the kennel runs can be conveniently constructed from welded mesh set in steel frames with steel side-partitions.

The 2m (6ft) metal door is made

of galvanised sheet-metal, steel framed, with an opening window at the top. The units can be built separately or else joined together in a row.

The main argument in favour of modular kennels is their speed of construction, their flexibility to meet individual needs as well as their relatively inexpensive removal to another site. You can get advice on cost and delivery from your local supplier.

Building with brick

The cost of kennels constructed of bricks or concrete blocks can best be obtained by giving details to a building company and asking for an estimate. The chief advantage of building this way is the flexibility of arrangements for light and ventilation, together with lower heat loss, which means that the kennels can remain cooler in summer but warmer in winter. Greater options for ventilation will cut down the incidence of damp or condensation. The sloping roof will serve to route the rainwater away from the runs.

Adequate drain-piping and drainage are essential. If you have converted existing land to kennels, you will have to deal with the question of drainage, which can be a problem, especially on flat land; particularly where there is no proper main-sewage system. You need

to install efficient drainage to remove the effluent. Make sure, too, that the runs have sufficient 'fall' so that water used in the cleaning process flows away easily. Ensure that suitably placed water-taps are available, with a sufficient length of hose for sluicing the runs.

Other important matters to which you must give consideration are: a dog kitchen, food storage, dog bedding and the safe disposal of garbage and excreta. Other major items will include artificial lighting, heating and some provision for whelping-down your bitches.

Taking these subjects in order, the dog kitchen should ideally be situated next to the kennel block, complete with mains hot and cold water, electricity and some form of heating which is non-flammable, such as overhead heating. The kitchen, which could be better described as a dog utility-room, will be equipped with a basin and draining-board, cupboards for storing drugs and medicines, freezer units for meat and metal bins for storage of dry complete foods and cereals.

Freezer-tops are useful as a work-surface, especially for setting up

Below: *Set in plenty of ground: a well-organised group of covered kennels and runs of the type often seen in Germany.*

feeding bowls. These should be purchased in different sizes, with large shallow bowls for puppies. You will need a table, preferably metal, to complete the work-surface if necessary.

It follows from all this that the dog utility-room should be sufficiently large to accommodate all these fittings, equipment and stores. The more space you make available for foods, for example, the more you can order at a given time from your supplier. The individual price of each bag of complete food in a large delivery will be considerably less than if you were to buy a few bags at a time. You might even be able to strike a deal with a supplier or suppliers of dog food to act as a sub-agent, so you can sell to the general public, thereby subsidising the cost of feeding your own dogs.

Rats

To store food you need space and protection from damp and vermin such as rats. The latter are dangerous to dogs, especially young puppies between the age of six to twelve weeks, because many rats carry the disease of leptospirosis, which is almost always fatal unless the dog has received the appropriate injection (see Chapter 2).

We have always found it useful to encourage a small colony of farm cats to take up residence. The cats will hunt down the rats and provide an effective deterrent — far safer than the attentions of the pest-control people, who only have to make one mistake in placing the rat-poison for you to lose dogs.

BEDDING

Dog bedding comes in various forms; we consider wood-shavings, which can be obtained from the nearest saw-mill, to be the best. It is warm, relatively free from insects or harmful mites and can be easily removed for disposal when soiled. Wood-shavings which have been baled in plastic sheeting are water-resistant, and may be stacked in the open, but are best covered with large plastic sheets to prevent the rainwater seeping into the bales. Shavings packed in sacks, whether of paper or of cloth, will of course need to be stored under cover, preferably not too far distant from the kennels.

You will also need to acquire a couple of steel wheelbarrows of the sort that builders use.

Garbage and excreta should be removed for disposal in an incinerator. Take care to separate the non-flammable items. Keep all newspapers, however, as they will be invaluable if you go in for breeding.

Whilst mentioning cleaning, you will require stout brooms made with nylon bristles for 'mucking out' and a strong but light steel shovel. Big, heavier brooms will be needed for sweeping runs. You will need metal water pails for the dogs, large enough to hold nine litres (two gallons) and thick plastic buckets for carrying water to the runs. After the plastic buckets have seen better days they can still find employment as 'muck-buckets', useful for removing small quantities of soiled material or excreta from the runs. A length of hose with a tap attachment will be required to sluice the runs. And disinfectant? We just use plain old-fashioned bleach diluted with water. It is cheap and very efficient. However, if you are using this make sure that no bleach pools are left as they are dangerous to dogs, especially puppies.

Windows and light

Top-hung window casements are the norm for kennel construction, but the window space needs to be filled with Perspex (*never* glass), as well as closely spaced metal bars or welded mesh. Dogs are very agile and readers need hardly be reminded of the dangers of contact between dogs in the kennel and dogs outside in the run. Without protection, unwelcome contact might take place, with consequent injuries such as torn ears and, in extreme cases, loss of life.

Additional lighting may be provided in the kennels, but for normal purposes natural light should be enough. Kennels for specialist use such as whelping or for the sick dog will require electric lighting. Outside lighting, however, should be installed and situated so that any shadows are eliminated. This is so that operations after dark can be carried out as efficiently as in daylight.

Heating of kennels is a difficult subject, and perhaps no perfect system has yet been evolved which is at once effective and economical to install and to operate. Underfloor heating and modern air-flow systems are expensive, whilst electric or infra-red heating elements can be dangerous unless well protected against an agile dog. Whichever system you select, it must meet with the necessary safety standards. For instance, in Great Britain, all dog breeders must be licensed by the Department of the Environment, whose task it is to ensure that the provisions of the appropriate legislation are fully complied with.

Below: *A kennel block of concrete and welded mesh construction. Notice the high partition walls for the safety of the dogs.*

DESIGN

In considering the design of your kennels, you may decide that a straight block would be ideal for your requirements. This is perfect if your kennel is to consist of just working dogs, that is to say males and spayed bitches. But if you intend to keep dogs and breeding bitches, as most of us do, then you will have a problem when your bitches come into season.

During these times the males will, naturally, pine for the bitches, and frustrated in their desires, may lose appetite and condition. The answer to this problem is either to split the block into two groups, away from one another, or to erect a few kennels for the purpose.

Whelping pen
If you do go in for breeding, then you will need a whelping pen. We have two main whelping pens, which is enough for our purposes as we rarely have more than two litters to deal with at any one time.

When not in use for breeding, whelping pens can be used for a sick dog. The pen keeps the dog in isolation, and at the same time near at hand so that attention can be given. Details of the whelping box are given in the next chapter.

THE STOCK

Now to the question of what sort of stock you should keep. Chapter 6, on breeding, will tell you more about the qualities needed by a breeding-bitch. Our advice is: stick to bitches, at least until your kennel is well established and you have the time to devote to the males. This needs an explanation, especially when one has to add that a fine, male adult German Shepherd with all the attributes needed to comply with the Standard, can and perhaps should represent the peak of achievement by any breeder. But consider this: the bitch is your capital; she is the means by which you will create your own stock.

The male, on the other hand, is a luxury, and unless he is a popular stud dog, or is required in the home kennel for a specific purpose, such as obedience trials or schutzhund, then he will become a 'passenger'. And if for this reason he becomes neglected in the organisation of the kennel, it may ultimately have a deleterious effect on his temperament and character. The exception is the male imported for his bloodlines and type.

German males

In most countries of the world including to a lesser extent the United States, imports are taking their place in breeding programmes and, in countries where it is allowed, in schutzhund trials. In fact the cream of stud work, for instance in Great Britain, goes to the imports from Germany, where to an ever-increasing extent the GSD community, and not always for the best reasons, has turned its back on the old British bloodlines. In this way, every country in the WUSV has virtually replaced its domestic bloodlines with those from Germany.

Now, in this respect, the United States certainly *is* the exception. It is a question of degree, but there are signs that America may ultimately go the same way as the other countries.

IMPORTING

If you wish to import, you will have to think of documentation; health checks for the dog; and in some countries quarantine.

For dogs imported to the United States, health checks are desirable at point of despatch, but are not mandatory at the receiving end. Canada requires a certificate of health to be issued before departure; the dog is checked again upon arrival. There are no quarantine regulations in either country.

Australia has very stringent import requirements. All dogs imported into Australia must spend six months in a quarantine station (usually British), unless, of course, the dog is imported from Britain itself, which is rabies free. This must be followed by a one-month period of residence before the dog can be shipped to Australia, where a further period of quarantine is required before the importer may receive his dog. Health checks are very strict. The dog must be clear of the bacteria known as *Brucella canis*. A check for leptospirosis must also be conducted at a government testing station, not less than 30 days before export.

A cautionary word about imports. If they are to be purchased direct from Germany, deal with breeders direct rather than intermediaries. Shepherds over two years should be angekört (breed-surveyed) and should have the 'A Stamp' for hips. Dogs between one and two years should also have the 'A Stamp'. Check that both parents are angekört, but it would be most unlikely if in present-day Germany they were not.

As an importer, yearly copies of the Körbuch will publish details of all dogs which are angekört. And remember, the SV has a vetting service for intending importers. You should make use of it. If you import from countries other than Germany, ensure you receive a certificate of good hips, because without this your import will have no value.

Chapter Six

BREEDING

Timing
Bloodlines
Pregnancy
The birth
The first days
Weaning

The decision whether or not to breed your GSD should be governed by a number of important factors.

To begin with you decided on a bitch when you bought your puppy. She came from a reputable breeder and had an excellent pedigree. Months passed, she grew into a lovely young bitch, and, when first taken to obedience classes, was much admired.

At nine months she had her first season, which is usual for a Shepherd, and at a year old she was X-rayed and found to have very good hips. (Most countries will X-ray at 12 months but in the United States it is from the age of two years.)

You have been told by several knowledgeable people that your bitch is a good specimen, of the correct proportions, dentition and temperament. Now that it has been confirmed that she also has good hips, your thoughts turn to the possibility of breeding a litter of puppies from her.

Accommodation
Your first consideration must be whether or not you have suitable accommodation for a litter. Your outside kennel might well be suitable provided that you have both light and heat sufficiently available, especially if it is to be a winter litter.

Other suitable places might be found in the garage or the conservatory, provided there is natural light and no draughts. Always remember that the puppies in your litter will grow quickly and so at about seven-eight weeks they will need a lot of space. Puppies can make a lot of noise and mess, so do not forget to consider possible neighbour problems.

If you are using your outside kennel, the structure mentioned in Chapter 5 makes a good basic whelping box. For added warmth and seclusion we add 1m (3ft) high removable plywood sides with a gap at one side — not facing a draught — big enough for the bitch to get in and out.

When you have finished with them, of course, the plywood sides can be easily stored away for the next time.

Also start to save up your newspapers, as these make excellent whelping beds.

TIMING

Spring is the best time for a litter, because the puppies will be ready to leave at the beginning of summer. Sales are also usually better at this time of year and the puppies will have the benefit of the summer weather for the first few months of their lives.

In hot climates you would be wise to choose the winter months so that the puppies can start their lives in cooler conditions and gradually get used to coping with excessive temperatures.

The cost
The cost of rearing and marketing must be carefully thought out. A litter, especially a large one, can be very expensive to rear, and if they have not been placed with new owners by eight weeks you will have the added cost of extra inoculations to consider. We give a leptospirosis/parvovirus inoculation, which overrides the bitch's immunity, at six weeks with a repeat at nine weeks. Puppies over 12 weeks can also be difficult to sell, so do make certain you have a good outlet for them.

When to mate
Your next consideration should be to decide at what age your bitch is to be mated. Many authorities suggest her third season, but if she has a season every four months, she would in our opinion be far too young. We prefer to wait until she is 21 months, which would make her nearly two years before she has a litter.

In Germany you cannot breed from a bitch until she has been X-rayed and passed her breed survey, this will be taken when she is two years of age.

Bitches vary considerably with

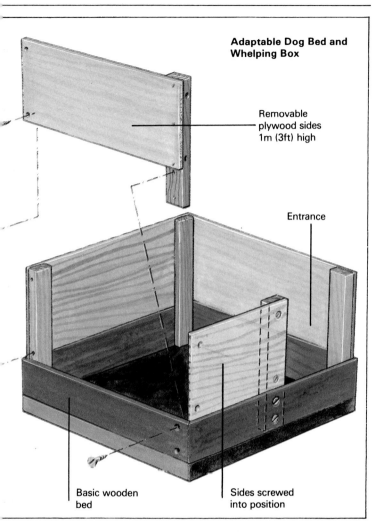

Adaptable Dog Bed and Whelping Box

Removable plywood sides 1m (3ft) high

Entrance

Basic wooden bed

Sides screwed into position

Above: *A typical bed and whelping box. The light plywood sides are attached with screws and are easily removable.*

regard to the interval between seasons. Most of ours have a four and a half to five month cycle rather than one of six months. Possibly the weather or time of year is a factor, as we have noticed that many of the bitches in our area seem to have the same cycle. This can result, two months later, in a glut of puppies, which isn't very

good for sales. If you intend to breed from your bitch, always take notes of the time and length of her seasons. This will give you an exact record as to the best time to mate her.

The days

We usually say that the twelfth day is the best for mating, but if your bitch is only in season for about 12-14 days then this of course will not apply.

We have had bitches ready to mate on the sixth or seventh day and others who would not let a dog near them until the sixteenth or seventeenth day. There are no hard and fast rules, but if careful records are kept, then at least you will know exactly how long your bitch will stay in season.

You may be told by some authorities that the right time is when the colour of her discharge starts to pale or ceases altogether, or if when you touch her back or hindquarters she puts her tail to one side. Doubtless all these methods have been successful at one time, but if you rely on them entirely, you may miss the right day completely.

The surest way is to try her with a dog (any breed will do) and see what her reactions are. If she flirts with him and puts her tail to one side then she is ready. How many of us, though, have a spare dog available? Our advice in these circumstances is that when booking the stud dog, you ask the owners which day they advise you to bring her along.

BLOODLINES

And now to the all important question of what dog to use. In a book of this size it is impossible to go into the details of bloodlines. These vary from one country to another but there are books on this subject which are both interesting and instructive to read.

The importance of choosing the right dog is that you have a GSD with an excellent temperament and very good hips so you do not want to take a backward step on these two points, both of which are so vital to the pet owners who will be buying most of your puppies.

By now, you should have studied the Standard carefully so that you have some idea of your bitch's proportions and type. Is she too long for her height, does she lack length of front leg or is she short in croup? What are her angles in fore- and hindquarters? How about colour, coat, ear carriage and dentition? The Standard is discussed elsewhere in this book and will give you guidelines to answer questions such as these.

Take notes on what you think needs improving. These should read something like this:
Temperament, hips, dentition. Correct
Colour. Paling — needs correction
Ears. Correct

Proportions
Body length — Too long. Needs correction
Front legs — Too short. Needs correction
Croup — Short and flat. Needs correction
Angles front and back. Correct

Movement
Side gait — Lacks forereach and hindthrust. Needs correction

Backline — Dip behind the withers. Needs correction
Action coming — Loose elbows. Needs correction
Action going away — Sound

So what conclusions do we come to? To begin with, we *must* have good temperament and good hips. Do not even consider a stud unless he has both of these. The stud's construction is the next consideration.

To correct the faults in our own bitch, we need a dog with:
A good height at the withers, derived from a well-laid shoulder
An upper arm of the correct length and angle
A hard back
A long, correctly angled croup
Tight in the elbows
Dark grey sable or predominantly black and gold in colour, to correct the bitch's paling

The dog must not only show these characteristics but must also be genetically capable of producing them. But where do you find such a dog?

Above right: *Ch. Cito vom Konigsbruch. A German import and top British sire since 1983. He is very prepotent for his type.*

Below: *Ch. Jonal Basko. A typical Ch. Cito son. Through his progeny, Cito has been responsible for an improvement of type.*

Bottom: *Ch. Gayville's Canti. A typical Cito daughter. Her sire has produced improved proportions, top lines and croups.*

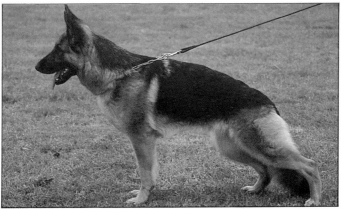

First of all contact the original breeders of your bitch and see what they have to suggest. Next, get in touch with the premier breed club in your country and ask for a list of breeders in your area. If any of these breeders have a dog of interest, with good hips, then go and see it.

Check his temperament and try to see some of his offspring. If he appears to be siring what you are looking for, then use him. If not, then look elsewhere and try again at another kennel.

If you allow yourself plenty of time before your bitch comes into season you need not rush to choose the right dog.

With the breeder's help, check the dog's pedigree for such undesirable hereditary problems as HD, bad temperament, epilepsy and haemophilia. If these check-out all right, then you have found the right dog, worthy of your bitch, who will give you the super litter you have planned for so carefully and for so long.

The expense and accommodation have all been sorted out, you have chosen your sire and have told his owner when your bitch is due in season.

The bitch's condition
Your next consideration is to make certain that the bitch is in tip-top condition so as to be able to cope with her litter.

Check that she is up to date with all inoculations, then worm her and make certain she is not carrying any external parasites. In America she will have to be checked for Brucillosis as most stud dog owners will not accept a bitch without a certificate of clearance. This will have to be done by your veterinary surgeon.

Some people will prescribe vitamin E tablets for increased fertility and raspberry leaf tablets for easy whelping. We have no proof that these work but they certainly will do no harm if you care to try them.

See that she is not carrying excess weight nor must she be too thin. For good condition, you want to be able to feel the ribs but not see them.

Mating
Your bitch has now come into season and you have rung the stud dog's owner and arranged a suitable day to take her. All travelling arrangements should have been carefully thought out and made in advance. We always travel with the bitch so as to keep her as relaxed as possible and avoid too much stress. You are far more likely to get a successful mating with a relaxed bitch than from one who is tense. Make certain that your bitch has a chance to relieve herself before the mating takes place.

It is usual for the bitch to go to the dog but sometimes, if the dog happens to be going to a nearby show, you might be able to meet up there. We like to be present at a mating so that if the bitch gets worried as, after all, this is a completely new experience for her,

Below: 'Franka' on her way to the stud dog. To keep your bitch relaxed, it is always a good idea to travel with her.

we are there to soothe her and give her confidence. A keen stud dog will usually mate quickly, especially if the bitch is ready, but sometimes you will find that she will struggle and try to get away. In cases like this, the owner of the stud dog will give you instructions on what you should do.

It is normal for the dog and bitch to 'tie' during mating and this may last for about 20 minutes. Although not strictly necessary, it is desirable as during this phase the dog is passing fluid into the bitch which will increase the possibility of conception.

As soon as the mating has been completed give your bitch a drink, though it is advisable not to let her urinate. One mating should be sufficient especially if there has been a good tie, but if the dog does not tie, try to arrange another the next day. This may not always be possible and then one must just trust to luck and hope for the best. On receipt of the stud fee, however, we always state to bitch owners that if the bitch should miss or only have a born-dead puppy, a free mating will be given to her on her next season.

Pregnancy

A bitch's pregnancy is usually reckoned to be 63 days from the date of the first mating but we have found that 60-61 days is the norm as far as our bitches are concerned.

Between the third and fourth weeks your vet, on examination, can usually tell whether she is in whelp or not. Sometimes with a maiden bitch she will not show any signs until the seventh or eighth week, especially if she is carrying a small litter.

During pregnancy, you might find your bitch becomes much more affectionate, she might go off her food or even be sick and possibly start digging holes in the garden. These are all signs of her being in whelp and should give you no undue concern.

From the sixth week onwards, we start increasing her food by giving an extra meal in the morning. If fed on a complete diet, it is now advisable to go back to one with a high protein content.

Below: *After the successful mating, the pregnancy follows its course. Here is 'Franka' now eight weeks in whelp.*

PREPARATIONS

A week or ten days before she is due, put her into the place or kennel that you have chosen for whelping. Put plenty of clean newspaper into her whelping box; as she comes nearer her time, she will scratch up and tear up the paper into small pieces.

You too must be ready for the event, so get together the things you might need:
A good stock of newspapers is essential
Two or three clean towels
A box of tissues
Sterile umbilical cord (as used medically — or simply use cotton)
Blunt-ended curved scissors
A small cardboard box
A set of scales to weigh the puppies (not essential)
Hot water bottle

Several days beforehand, she might go off her food but this is not a particularly reliable guide. Some bitches will eat heartily right up to the moment of birth. Some will show milk 14 days beforehand, others will not let any milk down until the first puppy has been born. It is best to play it by ear.

If she has not whelped before or on her due date, then we would ask the vet to check her to see that everything is in order. If at any time during her pregnancy your bitch has a dark green, or red, or pus-like, or anything other than a clear discharge, call your vet immediately as she might have a complication caused by a womb infection.

Quite a useful guide is a temperature check. Two to three days before whelping your bitch's temperature will start dropping from normal 38°C(101.2°F) down to around 37°C(98°F). This is to prepare the puppies to come into a cooler world and is a very good guide.

A few hours before actually giving birth, she will start to pant heavily and shiver. This is an indication of the commencement of labour pains. If you look at her vulva now you will notice that it has become swollen and soft and that there is a clear discharge. The shivering will be replaced by straining; slightly and then more pronounced and at closer intervals.

During this time she will be licking herself and possibly she might pass some pale green liquid. This is the water bag breaking and within an hour the first puppy should be born. If the bitch strains hard for longer than an hour, it is best to contact your vet as there is

a possibility she might have a complication such as a breech-birth, which means the puppy is coming the wrong way round. It may also mean that one puppy is dead and stopping the others.

THE BIRTH

The bitch then gives one almighty heave and out comes a puppy. It will probably still be in its bag and lying quite still. Your bitch will then get busy pulling out the afterbirth, breaking the cord and cleaning the puppy. It will be then that your firstborn will start to kick and gasp for breath. She will continue licking it vigorously and this will normally make it cry. We are always pleased to hear that cry as it means that the puppy's lungs have started to function properly.

When the bitch begins to clean herself, rub the puppy in a clean towel and put it on her to suckle. Put fresh newspaper under her and her puppy as usually you will find quite a lot of fluid has been passed. Sometimes a maiden bitch will not know what to do and will leave the puppy lying without making any attempt to clean it. In this case, we push her head down on to the cord and usually she will start to chew.

If there is still no reaction, after having thoroughly washed and disinfected our hands we gently ease out the afterbirth and then cut the cord at an angle about 5cm (2in) from the puppy's stomach. We then rub the puppy making certain that it has no membranes over its nose or in its mouth. By this time the bitch will usually have taken over and you can put the puppy on to a teat which it will soon be sucking vigorously.

If a puppy is born which, even after the bitch's attention, still shows no sign of life, rub it vigorously and shake it with its head down so as to get rid of any surplus fluid. If this fails, try mouth-to-mouth resuscitation by blowing air into the lungs, similar to that used for first aid in humans. When its breathing has started, put it into the cardboard box which you will have got ready beforehand with a hot water bottle well-covered in towels, so as to get it thoroughly warm and dry. Then give it back to its mother.

Offer her a drink of warm milk with

Below left: Older puppies need just as much care and attention as the newborn. Fresh water and clean bedding are essential.

Below: Puppies contentedly feeding from their mother at eight days. Notice how protective 'Wanda' is of her litter.

a little honey and leave her while you go and find some suitable beverage to revive yourself after your efforts at being a midwife!

The second
Your bitch, especially if she has a large litter, might have another puppy almost immediately after having the first. She might, of course, go longer, but if she shows no signs of straining within the next two hours phone the vet.

After an examination, he will decide what is best and will possibly give her an injection to bring her back into labour.

When the bitch starts to strain again, put the puppy or puppies into your prepared cardboard box so that they will not get wet when the next pup is born. Some bitches will not allow you to do this, in which case you must try, as far as possible, to keep them away from her rear end so that she can deal with her newborn without interruption from the others. Do not forget to offer the bitch a drink and to keep the whelping box dry with fresh newspaper.

Checking
You now have eight puppies, all suckling well. The exhausted mother looks happy, and you are pretty sure that she has finished whelping. Contented, you gaze down on your first efforts at breeding.

Have a pencil and pad handy to note down the times of birth as well as the weight and sex of each puppy. Check the puppies for hind dew-claws and any deformities. If hind dew-claws are present they will have to be removed within 48 hours of birth, which is a job for the vet or an experienced breeder. Front dew-claws are *not* removed from a GSD. Ask the vet to call to see your bitch to make sure she has no more puppies or any retained afterbirths.

The GSD is an easy whelper, getting on with the job quickly and efficiently, and we have described what we consider to be a normal whelping. Problems can occur

though and unless you are an experienced breeder they should be left to the vet. If, however, you live a long way from one, get an experienced breeder to help you.

The cord
There are just one or two other points worth mentioning. Your sterile umbilical cord will come in handy if a puppy's severed cord continues bleeding.

With the umbilical cord make two loops pulled tight and tied in a reef knot as close to the puppy's stomach as you can. This will soon stop the bleeding.

If whelping is prolonged take your bitch out and give her a chance to relieve herself. In cold weather, heating is necessary either with an infra-red lamp or underfloor heating. *Never* heat with an open flame as this can be highly dangerous.

TO BE PRESENT?

Some bitches like you to be with them throughout the whelping, others just like you to be around. Whichever it is, we never leave a bitch to whelp on its own as advocated by some people. Remember, should an awful choice have to be made, it is preferable to lose the puppy to the bitch.

Records

It is very important that you keep a thorough record of your bitch's pregnancy. Knowing exactly when she was mated and the length of her pregnancy will prove invaluable.

Below: *What all the work and planning is for. Here are a proud owner and mother with two puppies and their future owners.*

THE FIRST DAYS

For the first few days after whelping your bitch will prefer sloppy foods such as milk and a breakfast cereal, but gradually reintroduce her to a high protein diet, making certain it contains both vitamin supplements and calcium. Calcium and vitamin D are both very important, especially if your bitch has had a large litter.

While the bitch is producing milk (the time known as lactation), she should be fed as much as she likes three or four times daily. During this time make a point of feeling her milk glands every day. If any one of them feels hot and hard then she has probably developed mastitis. Contact the vet who will treat it with antibiotics.

If the bitch begins to have a bright red or thick, smelly, dark

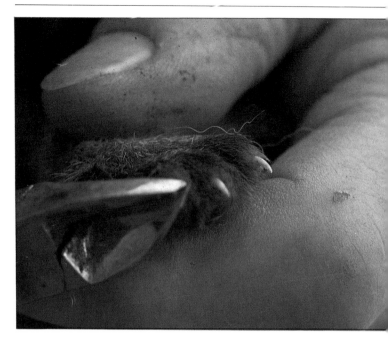

green discharge from her vulva, then call the vet immediately, as she might have complications such as a haemorrhage or metritis. Except for complications such as these, all discharge should be finished within seven days of whelping. (See also Chapter 7.)

Puppy care

Cut the puppies' nails with nail clippers or sharp nail scissors at around seven days. Cut them regularly after this as they become very sharp and make an awful mess of the bitch's teats. After a week the puppies will be moving about quite a lot and at 10-14 days their eyes will open. After this, the puppies begin to grow very quickly and their activity increases rapidly; the time has come to think about weaning them.

WEANING

If the litter is large, then we start weaning at 14 days, but if the bitch has a litter of four puppies or less, then she is perfectly capable of feeding them right up until 21 days.

We use a complete diet which starts with a weaning porridge. Put a little into a saucer and push the puppies' noses into it. You will find that they will lap it up hungrily. Start with two meals, then gradually increase to four daily meals.

We then gradually change over to a small-nut feed of 30% protein on which they remain until around 12 months of age.

At seven weeks of age, when the puppies are ready to leave, they will be eating four meals daily, each consisting of 85-115g (3-4oz), dry weight, of 30% protein nuts soaked in hot water.

Worming

The puppies are wormed with pills obtainable from the vet at between three-four weeks of age, again ten days later and then once more before they leave.

Once weaning has commenced, we cut the bitch's food intake. This will reduce her milk production which her puppies no longer need now that they are on solid food. When the puppies are five weeks of age she is taken away from them during the day, and at six weeks she is taken from them altogether.

Conditions
Always keep clean drinking water available for the puppies, and make sure that they get plenty of fresh air and sunlight. Shade, of course, must always be available, especially in hot climates.

At about five weeks we usually change the bedding to wood-shavings as, especially with a large litter, newspaper becomes inadequate and makes the puppies rather smelly.

At six weeks the puppies get their first inoculation (see Chapter 2 for details of inoculation procedures).

We have found this particular method of rearing to be most successful over the years. The diet we use is easy, clean and perfectly balanced and takes away the chance element which so often leads to occurrences of stomach ailments and other problems.

Left: *Cutting the nails on a puppy of ten days. Nails should be cut regularly to avoid damage to the mother.*

Below: *Gently holding a puppy of ten days. At this stage of development, the puppy's eyes are just beginning to open.*

Chapter Seven

HEALTH MATTERS

Parasites
Bone conditions
Digestive problems
General and first aid
Convalescence

The well-bred, well-reared Shepherd is a healthy animal and should give you many years of relatively trouble free life. So you might wonder why we have such a long list of ailments. This book is geared to the GSD novice, who, having enjoyed their first Shepherd, decides to start breeding. Most of the ailments listed are uncommon but still can occur, so we feel that future breeders should be made aware of them.

EYES

Shepherds have very few eye complaints.

a) Juvenile Cataract Uncommon. Appears at around eight-nine months of age and looks like a white film which gradually covers the whole eye. Can be operated on to improve vision. Is hereditary and so this Shepherd should not be bred from.

Below: *Inspecting the eyes of a puppy. Fortunately the German Shepherd is prone to only a few eye complaints.*

b) Pannus Uncommon. A form of corneal inflammation which affects both eyes and is characterised by a pink or pigmented membrane growing across the cornea. Can result in blindness.

c) Conjunctivitis An inflammation of the conjunctiva which can be caused by mechanical agents and viruses as well as bacteria. A pus-like discharge and sometimes an inflamed third eyelid. Bathe with cold water or a dilute solution of boric acid made up for opthalmic use, obtainable from a pharmacy. If there is no improvement within 48 hours consult your vet.

d) A clear discharge is usually a sign of a foreign body in the eye such as grass seeds, dust etc. This can be urgent if the problem is a grass seed. Treat as for conjunctivitis.

SKIN PROBLEMS

Sometimes, especially when casting its coat, you will notice your dog scratching and biting, showing obvious signs of irritation. First check for parasites.

a) Wet Eczema If the skin is red

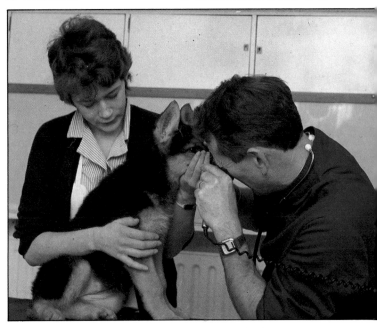

and looks wet and raw, with pus-like crusts, it is probably wet eczema. Treat with sulphur-based ointment, but if it continues then a visit to the vet is indicated. He will probably give an injection or pills to help.

Some dogs are allergic to straw so if you are using this for bedding try changing to shavings or newspaper.

b) Cysts When grooming your dog you will find small hard lumps which, when squeezed, emit hard, string-like pus. When empty, dab with disinfectant. They will often disappear as quickly as they appeared.

c) Interdigital Cysts Pus-filled lumps appearing in between the toes, which burst but usually reappear again, are painful and can cause lameness. Try hot fomentations, dry and then dust with an antiseptic powder. If they continue consult your vet.

With all the above, a change of diet is indicated. Cut out carbohydrates, especially flaked maize. Include garlic in the diet as this is an excellent blood purifier.

d) Ringworm This is caused by a fungus and is contagious, so isolation is essential. All bedding should be burnt and the kennel thoroughly scrubbed with disinfectant. You will see rapidly spreading bare patches which can occur on any part of the body. Clip hair round edges and treat with a fungistatic solution. If there is no improvement consult your vet who will prescribe a suitable drug, which given by mouth or injection will soon cure it.

e) Mange (Sarcoptic) Your dog will be persistently scratching and roughened bare patches will appear around the elbows, stifles, ears and eyes. Bathe every seven days until cured with a skin bath prescribed by your vet.

f) Mange (Demodectic) Bare patches appear round the eyes, nose, legs and feet. There is little or no scratching. The patches have a peculiar smell. Go straight to the vet as this is very difficult, sometimes impossible, to cure.

Modern remedies, however, offer a good chance, especially if treatment is started early.

PARASITES (EXTERNAL)

a) Fleas and Lice These are not difficult to get rid of and in a well run, clean kennel should not occur. Fleas breed off the dog and are the host of some tapeworms. Bathe the dog in a shampoo containing an insecticide and then spray with an anti-flea preparation. There are several good ones available. If fleas are a problem, spray the dog regularly also including its living quarters. Burn all bedding.

b) Ticks Anybody living in the country especially where there are sheep or deer, will, sooner or later, find a tick on their dog. Do not pull it off, as, if the head remains in the skin, it can cause a nasty sore. Cut the tick in half with a sharp pair of scissors; the head should then drop off. If this does not work, try dowsing it with surgical spirit. If you live in a hot country or an area which is tick infested, dip your dog once a week in a bath containing a tick-killing insecticide. In hot climates flies bite around the ears causing the dog great discomfort. Consult your vet on a suitable spray to control this.

PARASITES (INTERNAL)

a) Roundworm Usually found in young puppies. If the puppy looks thin or bloated this can sometimes be the cause. Worm with a preparation containing a suitable vermifuge and repeat ten days later.

b) Tapeworm Can be found in dogs of any age, but unusual in very young puppies. You will see segments, which look like grains of rice, in the motions and round the anus. Dose, carefully following instructions, with a tapeworm preparation. The presence of hookworm, heartworm, threadworm etc is diagnosed by a faeces test. Your vet will then prescribe the right treatment. If your dog has a voracious appetite but still remains in poor condition, has a staring coat or blood in the motions, but otherwise appears normal, worms could be one cause.

POISONS

The most common are Warfarin, used in rat and mouse bait, lead and metaldehyde found in slug bait. If you suspect your dog has eaten any of these try to induce vomiting by pushing a lump of washing soda down its throat and get to the vet as quickly as possible. If you can, tell him what type of poison you suspect your dog has eaten.

BONE CONDITIONS

a) Hip Dysplasia is by far the most common condition. This is caused by a malformed femur head (thigh bone) failing to fit into a shallow acetabulum (hip socket) thus causing partial or complete dislocation. In severe cases the dog will have great difficulty in walking and getting up. However, there are many degrees of this complaint and a GSD with minor or moderate HD is perfectly capable of leading a normal active life. As this is a hereditary complaint, no dog can be described as being 'free' or 'clear' as it is impossible to know what its genetic make-up is. On no account should a badly dysplasic Shepherd be used in a breeding programme. In most countries in the world there is a hip scheme. Hip dysplasia can only be correctly diagnosed by X-ray. A GSD with moderate or severe HD is unsuitable for working trials or any other activity where prolonged gaiting or jumping is required. In bad cases the surgical removal of the femur head has been reasonably successful, also an operation called pectineal nyotomy which involves cutting the pectineal muscle on one or both sides of the inner thigh. Hip replacement is also very successful, but expensive.
b) Ununited Anconeal Process, commonly referred to as elbow dysplasia or nonfusion of the elbow joint, is a condition caused by a

---

Common Dog Parasites

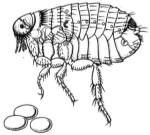

Dog flea *(Ctenocephalides canis)*

Dog tick *(Ixodes ricinus)*

Dog louse *(Linognathus setosus)*

Follicular mite *(Demodex canis)*

faulty union of the anconeal process (one of the elbow bones) with the ulna. The loose fragment of bone sets up irritation in the elbow joint. This first becomes noticeable at five-six months. The dog will display intermittent lameness and you will notice a thickening on the outside of one or both elbow joints and the feet and pasterns will turn outwards.

This can only be diagnosed by X-ray. The most effective treatment is surgical removal of the loose piece of bone. This condition is believed to be hereditary but not very common.

Below: *On the left hand side can be seen four external dog parasites, while on the right hand side (below) are four common types of internal parasite:*
1 Roundworm (Toxocara canis)
2 Tapeworm (Dipylidium caninum)
3 Whipworm (Trichuris vulpis)
4 Hookworm (Ancylostoma caninum)

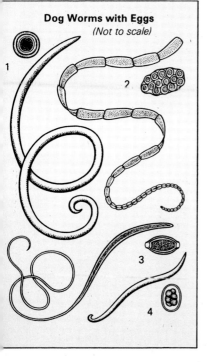

Dog Worms with Eggs
(Not to scale)

1
2
3
4

c) Chronic Degenerative Radiculo Myeopathy (CDRM)
Can be seen in the middle aged Shepherd but is a condition of the elderly.

CDRM or Chronic Degenerative Radiculo Myeopathy, is often the cause of the elderly Shepherd losing the use of its hind legs. It is a condition which is in no way connected with HD. First signs are lameness in one or both hind legs and visible muscle wastage. Finally the Shepherd becomes completely paralysed in both hind legs, is unable to stand and becomes incontinent.

There is no pain attached to this condition except the mental anguish which some dogs undoubtably feel at their immobility. In every other respect they are mentally and physically fit.

So far little research has been done into this condition so there appears to be no cure — euthanasia is perhaps the only answer.

CONDITIONS OF YOUNG PUPPIES

a) Oesophagus, Aortic Arch Anomolies, Pyloric Stenosis, are all causes of regurgitation of food in young puppies when first started on a solid diet, at weaning or shortly after.

The aortic arch is a retained foetal artery which produces outside pressure on the oesophagus making solid food unable to pass into the stomach. When this happens, the oesophagus forms a bag in front of the stomach in which the solid food collects and is unable to pass into the stomach. This can sometimes happen when the aortic arch has not been retained.

Pyloric Stenosis has similar symptoms but in this case the food is unable to pass from the stomach into the intestines.

All the above can only be correctly diagnosed by a vet, after various tests have been made. We feel that in all cases euthanasia is the best answer. All are relatively uncommon but anybody intending to breed should be aware of their existence. These conditions can sometimes be surgically corrected.

b) Hernia If the mother has been over enthusiastic in severing the cord, you will sometimes find a small lump remains. If the intestine is protruding, your vet will close the gap with a couple of stitches, though in a young puppy this is not always successful because of shock and infection. Umbilical hernia can be hereditary.

c) Intussusception Describes a situation in which the bowel telescopes in upon itself. Usually caused by excessive vomiting and diarrhoea. Surgery is usually successful if diagnosed early.

BITCH CONDITIONS

a) Metritis Inflammation of the womb which usually occurs within a week of whelping. The bitch becomes listless, sometimes will start straining again and often fever will set in. Consult your vet immediately who will give a course of antibiotics which will soon clear up this condition.

b) Pyometra A much more serious infection of the womb, which in this case becomes filled with pus. An immediate hysterectomy is the only solution. Can be fatal if not dealt with immediately. Sometimes older bitches develop this three or

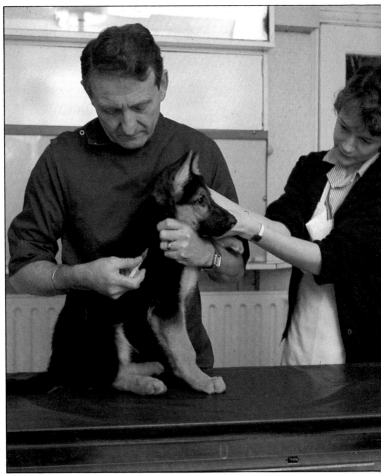

four weeks after finishing a season.

c) Vaginitis This is an inflammation of the vagina and can also occur during puberty. The bitch will lick herself and urinate a lot. A vaginal douche and antibiotics will soon correct this.

d) Mastitis Discussed in Chapter 6.

e) Eclampsia Sometimes occurs in a bitch who has had a big litter and is being deprived of calcium, due to her inability to mobilise it quickly enough. She will start to stagger, look glassy eyed and then collapse. Immediate veterinary attention is essential or else this condition will prove fatal. Your vet will give a calcium injection and your bitch will quickly return to normal.

VIRAL AND BACTERIAL INFECTIONS

Most of the serious infections of this nature are covered by inoculations, and have been explained in Chapter 2.

a) Kennel Cough (Parinfluenza) This can take a variety of different forms. All forms are highly contagious and are best treated by your vet. A good cough mixure — there are many available — can help relieve the sore throat.

b) Tonsillitis This is a bacterial infection and, in an acute form, fever can occur. Treatment with antibiotics usually effects a cure. Feed on a liquid diet and keep the dog warm and quiet.

c) Pneumonia An inflammation of the lungs usually caused by a bacterial infection but can also be caused by shock and viruses. The dog's breathing becomes shallow and laboured, and you can hear a bubbling sound if you put your ear close to its chest. The dog will usually have a high temperature (about 40°C/104°F). Keep warm, especially the chest area. An old cardigan or pullover can be very useful in these cases. Put the front

legs down the sleeves and use safety pins to make it fit snugly around the chest and abdomen. Plenty of fresh air is desirable provided the dog is kept warm. Your vet will probably prescribe a broad spectrum antibiotic.

d) Brucellosis A bacterial infection which can cause abortion and also fading puppies. In many countries a clearance certificate is required before a bitch will be accepted for mating.

e) Nephritis This is inflammation of the kidneys, often caused by an infectious agent. The dog may drink a lot of water and urinate a lot. Older dogs can also suffer from this and we have found herbal remedies very useful as treatment. Barley water, made by boiling pearl barley for 30 minutes or soaking flaked barley overnight and then straining, is the best form of drinking water for a dog suffering from this condition. Your vet will prescribe an antibiotic.

DIGESTIVE PROBLEMS

a) Gastro Enteritis This covers a variety of bowel conditions, the symptoms of which are sickness and diarrhoea. Enteritis is the inflammation of the bowel and in a mild form it is quickly cured by kaolin-based medications. Starve for two days, giving only small drinks of honey and water. This gives the bowel a chance to heal and also slows down the whole digestive system.

If the dog passes or vomits blood and has a temperature your vet will prescribe a broad spectrum antibiotic. After a serious attack of enteritis, pancreatic deficiency or malabsorption problems can occur. A faeces or blood test is required to ascertain whether either is present. These two problems, believed by some to be hereditary, may be the answer to your dog's poor condition in spite of eating well. Soft mud or grey coloured greasy motions are classic symptoms. With both these complaints the digestive system is not absorbing all the food, hence

Left: A method of inoculation. It is vital that your puppy receives the full range of inoculations necessary for its good health.

the poor condition. Once diagnosed, tablets are given which help to control this problem but the dog must be kept on a very bland diet such as rice and boiled chicken. In some cases it is incurable but controllable.

BLEEDING COMPLAINTS

Haemophilia and Von Willebrands Disease

There are several hereditary bleeding complaints of which these two are sometimes found in the GSD. The affected animal will bleed at the slightest provocation and the haemorrhage is very difficult to control.

a) Haemophilia Only males are affected but females are the carriers, so if your bitch produces a haemophilic dog immediately discard her and any of her offspring from your breeding programme. The male can be slightly or seriously affected and if you own a dog bred from a line known to have produced it, it is wisest to have blood tests taken.

b) Von Willebrands Disease Is an autosomal disease of incomplete dominance. It can occur in either sex. The type of bleeding is different, mainly surface and gums etc. America is affected by Von Willebrands so before buying a puppy in the USA, try to make sure that its parents and its pedigree are clear of the disease.

EPILEPSY

This is a most distressing complaint. Not all convulsions are hereditary of course, they can be caused by a blow on the head, brain tumour and the after-effects of distemper. In a convulsion the dog becomes rigid, starts shaking its head, rolling its eyes, champs its jaws usually producing a lot of

Below: *Listening for the heartbeat. Notice where the vet has placed the stethoscope on this adult Shepherd.*

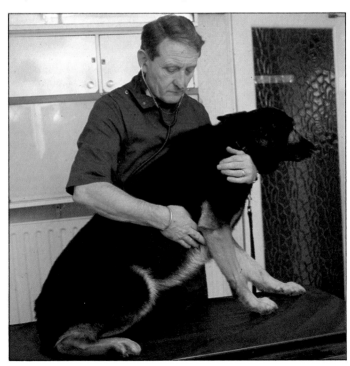

frothy white saliva. It will then fall on its side, its legs making galloping actions and often lose control of its bowels and bladder. The shaking will gradually subside and it will get back on to its feet but look rather dazed and be unsteady. The attack will be over in about two – three minutes. Talk soothingly to the dog but do not get your hand anywhere near its mouth. The only way to find out whether this is idiopathic (hereditary) epilepsy or not is for your vet to give it a thorough clinical examination and a brain reading taken with an encephalograph. This condition can be controlled by various anti-convulsant drugs. Do not breed from an affected animal. In a serious case of epilepsy where the dog is fitting very frequently euthanasia is the kindest solution. Can commence at any age but most commonly seen between the age of one and three years.

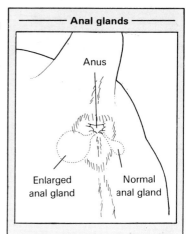

Anal glands

Anus

Enlarged anal gland

Normal anal gland

The dog's anal glands lie just below the skin on either side of the anus. They normally empty themselves when a motion is passed. Should they become full and the dog suffer discomfort, then consult your veterinary surgeon.

GENERAL AND FIRST AID

a) Cuts must be carefully cleaned and disinfected. If jagged and very open, it is best to have it stitched by the vet. If bleeding profusely first make certain it is not an artery (this would be bright red and pumping), bandage firmly with a pressure pad and leave for the blood to coagulate. Do not remove the dressing too soon as you could start the wound bleeding again. If a small wound dust with antiseptic powder and leave. If an artery has been severed, put on a tourniquet in between the wound and the heart and take immediately to the vet. Never leave a tourniquet on for more than 20 minutes. Release for a few minutes so as to allow blood into the limb again.

Liquid plastic skin dressing applied to cuts on pads is very helpful for quick healing.

b) Broken bones need immediate veterinary attention.

c) Lameness can be caused by a strained muscle or tendon. Keep the dog quiet with a minimum amount of exercise. If this does not improve within a few days seek expert veterinary advice.

d) Teeth If your dog develops smelly breath or starts pawing its mouth or rubbing it along the ground, you can suspect tooth problems. Sometimes, in older dogs, ulcers and bad teeth can occur. These can be extracted if necessary by a veterinary surgeon, but a general anaesthetic is necessary. A weekly marrow bone or hard biscuit will keep the teeth clean and in good condition. If you find them getting dirty, persuade your dentist to let you have an old teeth scaler and gently scrape the teeth but be careful not to damage the gums. If your dog is uncooperative a visit to the vet is indicated.

e) Anal Glands Two glands situated on either side of the anus. If the dog is producing good firm stools the anal glands will usually be emptied. If you notice your dog rubbing its bottom along the ground it is probably due to the anal glands. Get your vet to show you how to empty them — it is not too difficult, just a case of squeezing in the right place!

99

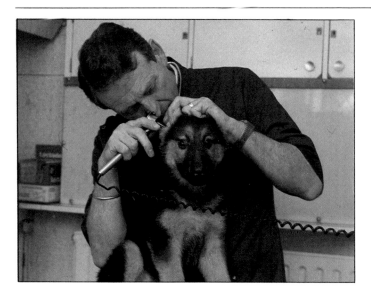

f) Ears Examine these regularly to make certain they are clean and free from wax. Calamine lotion is excellent for cleaning ears. Soak a tissue in it and then clean. If the wax is a dark reddish colour there is an infection. Your vet will give you an ointment to put in the ear night and morning which will soon clear this up. If the ear is sore and has a pus-like, smelly discharge, your dog is suffering from otitis (canker). Professional advice is best sought in this case.

g) Constipation A dessertspoon of liquid paraffin should do the trick but if it persists and the dog keeps on straining a blockage of the bowel can be suspected. Seek veterinary advice.

h) Feet Check to see that nails are kept short and trim with nail cutters if necessary. Be careful not to cut the quick, which will bleed.

i) Thorns These can be painful and sometimes very hard to remove. Soften the surrounding area by applying a hot compress and then extract with tweezers. Dab with disinfectant, dry carefully and dust with antiseptic powder. Make certain you have got rid of all the thorn.

j) Stomach Torsion or Bloat. This is a horrible complaint. It is caused by the stomach twisting over on its

Above: *Examining the ears. You should make a regular check of your dog's ears for wax or the start of infection.*

axis thus stopping the gases from dispersing by either mouth or bowels. Usually associated with excessive exercise after a heavy meal.

The stomach becomes completely distended and immediate veterinary attention must be sought. The vet will operate and return the stomach to its normal position. If this is not done quickly this condition will prove fatal. Can occur again.

k) Heat Stroke This is an emergency which requires immediate attention. Dogs left in cars, tied up in the full sun, or left in concrete runs without suitable shade can all develop heat stroke. Special care must be taken to provide shade for your dog when living in hot climates. Heat stroke starts with rapid, frantic breathing. The tongue and mucous

Right: *The correct way to take a dog's temperature. The thermometer can be smeared with Vaseline to help entry.*

membranes are bright red and the dog will start staggering. Put it in a tub of cold water or hose down with a garden hose. It is imperative to bring the temperature down as quickly as possible or this will prove fatal. Ice packs around the body (packets of frozen food can be used) will also help.

l) Stings If your GSD has been stung by a wasp, bee etc remove the sting where possible and give antihistamine tablets. If the sting is on the eye or tongue and there is excessive swelling, consult your vet immediately.

CONVALESCENCE

This is one of the most important parts of nursing a sick dog, as, without great care, the dog can relapse back into the former condition. When starvation has been necessary, give only small quantities of boiled water or saline solution as, with all fevers and enteritis, great care must be taken with diet. First of all offer liquids, then gradually commence solid food starting with natural yoghurts, scrambled eggs and then fish, chicken or rabbit. Great care must be taken to ensure that all bones have been removed. Feed small quantities and, as cereal, use boiled brown rice. The dog is in a weak state having used all its resources to combat the illness so it does not want its digestive system overloaded. Never mind how thin the dog looks, by very slowly getting it back on to its normal diet it will

soon regain condition. Watch the motions very carefully and if there is any looseness you will know you are going too fast. Convalescent diets can also be obtained from your vet.

Check the temperature regularly by inserting a blunt ended thermometer, smeared in Vaseline, into the rectum. The normal temperature of a dog is 101.2°F. Warmth is essential but not excessive heat. Keep the dog as quiet as possible but at the same time give it plenty of comfort and reassurance. As its condition improves allow it gentle exercise; this is most important in cases of broken bones and strains. In cases of lameness (strain, pulled ligaments and muscles) give 200mg. Vitamin C (ascorbic acid) daily. We have found this treatment most useful.

Suggestions for First Aid Requirements
Adhesive tape
Antihistamine tablets (for stings)
Antiseptic dusting powder
Aspirin
Bandages (selection)
Calamine lotion
Cough mixture
Cotton wool
Curved scissors
Disinfectant
Ear ointment (from vet)
Eye ointment (from vet)
Gauze
Honey
Kaolin (for upset stomachs)
Liquid paraffin
Nail clippers
Plastic skin dressing
Thermometer
Tweezers
Vaseline
Washing soda

The above items are useful things to have handy for everyday use, but you will find that you will build up your own first aid requirements, as so much depends on your own country, climate and distance from stores and veterinary surgery.

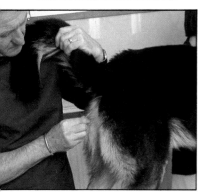

Chapter Eight

SHOWING YOUR GSD

The cost
Behaviour problems
The right formula
Breed Standard

Having made up your mind that you want to exhibit, you will have to decide what stock to buy. You could purchase a puppy of seven or eight weeks and then try it out in the puppy classes at a show when it is old enough. The question is: how certain can you be that it will win? However good the breeder may be at assessing potential, there is no way that he or she can guarantee a future winner. It is difficult enough to assess what an eight-week-old puppy will look like when it is old enough to show, say at six months.

Faults which do not come to light until the puppy is at least six months include incorrect dentition and chronic ear carriage (ie non erect). Other 'hidden' faults include 'non-entirety' (ie when one or both testicles in the male have not descended into the scrotum). A practical rule is to reject any puppy for showing if it is not already entire at eight weeks. If you decide to take a chance with an otherwise promising puppy, then you cannot complain later if you purchase the puppy as seen. Beware of bland assurances that the testicles will descend later on. Always seek the breeder's opinion in regard to such matters as entirety, dentition and ear carriage.

In an eight-week-old puppy, you can also obtain some idea of the 'bite'. Even at this age the top incisors should fit neatly over the bottom incisors in a scissor action. The ears should indicate some evidence of lift from the base. Beware of absolutely flat ears in a young puppy; these may be of a thin texture and may never become erect unless assisted.

Infrequent faults
You should not imagine, however, that these faults are widespread. Thankfully, their occurrence is quite infrequent. A Shepherd will have little chance in the showring unless it has a correct scissor bite, complete dentition and firm, well-placed, erect ears. The coat should be correct — that is to say it should not be too long, too coarse or silky

and should include underwool. Finally, it should not be one of the prohibited colours, such as white or near white.

So what should the would-be exhibitor do? Fortunately there is an alternative solution: you could buy older stock of six months or over, preferably with a convincing win to its credit, such as a high placing at a championship show in good competition under a reputable judge. You could also, of course, acquire an unshown puppy of six months, at least then you will see what you are getting.

In a puppy of this age, the ears should be up and the dentition can be examined to see if the bite is correct. All the teeth should be present. Sometimes one or another of the first premolars will be a little late in coming through, but you should be able to detect a slight bump in the gum indicating that the tooth is on its way.

THE COST

You must realise, however, that as soon as you start thinking about older stock, the purchase price will be much higher. Also the difference between the price of a show winner and an unshown puppy, even if that puppy is very promising, could be dramatic, unless you are very lucky and obtain a winner for a bargain price.

The reason for this price difference is obvious. On the one hand you are buying the puppy with a 'warranty', ie a good show win or wins. With an unshown puppy you are relying solely on your own judgement and that of the vendor, if you are wise enough to ask him.

Console yourself with the thought that most breeders will not attempt to sell a puppy of this age unless it has promise. They run on promising stock either for their own purposes or for sale to an exhibitor or for export.

It is not so easy selling an older puppy of six months or over to the public as a pet. To begin with the price will very likely be prohibitive, and in any case, the majority of pet owners prefer the experience of rearing a puppy 'from the nest' and moulding it to their own lifestyle.

Problems at a year

Never entertain the purchase of stock more than a year old, unless is has certified good hips. This means a low score under the BVA/GSDL scheme or an 'A Stamp' if it is a German import.

As the American OFA scheme

Below: *1984/5 Sieger Uran v. Wildsteigerland. An outstanding producer, he represents the best of the Canto/Quanto/Mutz bloodlines.*

does not apply until stock is two years of age, buyers will obviously have a problem.

The way round this is to ask your veterinarian to take hip X-rays and have them interpreted and assessed. There is no reason why you cannot obtain a good idea of the standard of hips in this way. You will need the cooperation of the vendor and, most importantly, the deliberations of an expert scrutineer, otherwise the exercise will be of little use.

The theory

Now to the Standard. You must read it through carefully and then refer to the illustration of the bone structure and anatomy of the German Shepherd. Get to know, for instance, what the croup is and where to find it. Learn about body proportions, height and the angles of the bones as well as their relative length. Do not cram: you are not taking a test. That may come later if you wish to become a judge.

For the moment, read the text, look at the diagram and study photographs of good dogs, then go and see some dogs at a show. After studying the theory, you should have a good idea about what a correct German Shepherd should look like. Beware of those who wish to impose their own ideas on you. In the canine world, where you are free to make your own decisions, always choose the right path — the path of the Standard — and do not deviate.

But which Standard to study? In this book we have printed the WUSV/FCI Standard as used by the GSD Breed Clubs in Great Britain. This Standard is one of the most detailed available, clearly stating preferences with regard to coat and colour as well as to the angles ideal for both croup and pastern.

Countries under the jurisdiction of the FCI are required to use the breed standard of the country of origin, and while not bound by FCI rules, Britain has chosen to come into line and has voluntarily adopted the WUSV/FCI Standard.

The British version, however, differs in some respects from the SV (German) version and it is worthwhile to detail exactly what these differences are.

The British version

To begin with, a stipulation appears in the SV version to the effect that the GSD should only be judged by specialists. No such clause exists in the British version on the principle that it is no good imposing a rule which cannot be enforced.

For while it is true that Breed Societies in Britain, Australia and the United States generally choose specialists to judge their shows, most all-breed shows and other competitions for awards in the Working or Herding group will be by necessity judged by all-rounders Likewise in Germany, the grade of 'V' or 'excellent' can only be awarded to a German Shepherd who has passed a test for temperament and gun-shyness and is in possession of a 'schutzhund' qualification, while elsewhere it is not a mandatory qualification for the attainment of such top breed awards as 'champion'.

Characteristics

You will notice that a great deal of space is given over to a description of characteristics and appearance of the German Shepherd. This section is very important because it defines the temperament and character as well as the breed's physical characteristics. Perhaps the key words to be understood and remembered are 'steadiness of nerves' — 'loyalty' — 'self-assurance' — 'courage' — 'tractability'.

This last characteristic is perhaps a little difficult to grasp and needs some kind of explanation.

In the context of what the Standard stipulates it means that the dog should be easily handled and manageable. The German Shepherd certainly should not be nervous, over-aggressive or shy. These are looked on as very serious faults in the German Shepherd Dog.

BEHAVIOURAL PROBLEMS

Despite attempts to formulate a perfect temperament for the breed, some behavioural problems have existed and have given rise to public criticism. The introduction of modern bloodlines from Germany, where we have seen far more controlled breeding, has done much to improve the temperament and character of the breed. But as we have seen earlier in this book, there is more to breeding than just putting a dog and bitch together. Breeders must use the best available material to avoid the pitfalls which arise from ignorance of the genetic background.

The WUSV/FCI preference

The media of many countries have for the most part cast the GSD as an 'attack dog'. With this in mind, the Breed Societies of Britain, conscious that breeders vary in knowledge, skill and motivation, have requested the removal of any reference to 'offensive' as opposed to 'defensive' traits in the Standard. This has been done with the full agreement of the SV and the WUSV.

In this way the Standard requires the German Shepherd to, "defend

Above: *1986/7 Sieger Quando v. Arminius, half brother to Uran. He represents the peak of excellence in the German Shepherd Dog.*

his master and his master's property". This puts the character of the dog into a correct perspective. If it is properly bred and reared, the German Shepherd will form a loving and affectionate relationship with family and friends. It will establish a respectful attitude towards visitors to the home territory, and will protect the family against intruders of whatever kind; just as they protected the flocks, as they still do.

Most other English-speaking countries, have elected to adopt the SV (German) version of the WUSV/FCI Standard as a 'blueprint' for the ideal GSD.

The American Standard

The Americans, though members of the WUSV, have their own Standard. It is very good in some sections, though in areas such as coat and colour it does lack some detail.

In the same way, some angles such as the croup, neck and shoulder are omitted together with certain proportions.

While a 'deep bodied dog' is called for, no mention is made of the fact that the chest should be 45-48% of the height at the wither.

Length to height proportions are set at 10-8½, in comparison with the WUSV/FCI Standard which calls for a dog with a ratio of 8½-9 height to 10 length.

On the subject of height, the US Standard also differs from that of the WUSV/FCI. In America no ideal height is given: dogs should be 24in-26in, bitches 22in-24in.

The WUSV/FCI Standard calls for an ideal height of 62.5cm for dogs and 57.5cm for bitches. A leeway of 2.5cm above or below the norm is allowed.

It could be argued that the American Standard allows for oversize dogs, until of course one remembers that in this version, height is measured to the point of the shoulder and not to the wither, as is the case in the WUSV/FCI Standard.

In our opinion, the American Standard for the German Shepherd, though very descriptive in its own way, does lack a degree of precision. This clearly gives breeders and judges much more scope and opportunity for individual interpretation than is certainly the case in other countries in the orbit of the WUSV.

Above: *A good example of an all-black German Shepherd. A colour permitted by the Standard and favoured by some people.*

The SV shows

The WUSV has promoted the concept that a dog show is not just a competition to select the most beautiful dog and declare a winner. To WUSV thinking, the dog show forms an integral part of the system for breed improvement.

In Germany, SV judges are fully trained and must pass a series of examinations on every aspect of the German Shepherd. At SV shows and in WUSV countries where the regulations of the national kennel club permit, the judge will place each dog in the class into a breed category or grade from 'Very Good' to 'Faulty'. The grade of 'Excellent' is reserved for dogs over two years of age.

At SV shows the dog must be in possession of good hips and a working (ie Schutzhund) qualification. At the Sieger or Main-Breed Show (Hauptzuchtschau) the dog must also pass a courage test and a test for 'steadiness to the gun'. The grade awarded will be entered on the dog's personal dossier and will appear on official pedigrees together with other information, the most important of which is the breed-survey category and the critique of the Breedmaster (Körmeister) on the parents and grandparents. A full report on surveyed dogs can be found in the various issues of the Breed Survey Book (Körbuch).

One should not imagine, however, that showing German Shepherds under such a system is a dull business, where the exhibitor is merely a cog in a machine for gathering breed information. Anyone who has been to a show in Germany — especially the Sieger Show — will know that it is, on the contrary, a very exciting event where the dogs are really put through their paces.

Included are long walking and gaiting sessions, enabling any spectator to get a really good look at the dogs over a period of time — in the case of the Sieger Show over three days. The judges in these shows must make sure that the dogs demonstrate by their correctness of build, their stamina and their alertness, that they can function properly as working dogs.

Joining a society

The importance of joining your local and national breed society cannot be urged strongly enough. Through contact with the society you will discover a great deal about the show-scene in your particular country. Having read your Standard, studied some photographs of good dogs and visited some shows, you will perhaps have formed an idea of what the judge is looking for, as demonstrated by his or her placings. You may also have gained some insight into the way handlers, particularly the top handlers, get the best out of their dogs. Learn the 'mechanics' of handling the German Shepherd at a local training club and, if possible, gain some experience at the smaller shows.

It will soon become apparent that certain dogs are doing the winning. You must at this point ask yourself the question: are the winning dogs

always the best dogs? The answer to that question in our view comes only with practical experience: look, listen and learn. Cultivate an enquiring mind, but do not air your views until you really know what you are talking about. With this approach, much hard work, a modicum of talent and a little luck, you could go a long way.

THE RIGHT FORMULA

The Standard we have chosen is a good formula for a compact, athletic, balanced dog of good proportions: slightly longer than it is high, whose depth of body is slightly less than half its height. With leg bones of the correct length and angle and with correct musculature, such a dog can perform the unique long-striding, endurance gait which enables a German Shepherd to travel all day if it has to. The Standard is in fact the formula for an all-purpose working dog.

Such a dog has the power to scale a high wall and the length of leg to move over rough ground. Erect, forward-placed ears give acute hearing while the clean muzzle aids scenting ability. Despite these marvellous physical advantages, however, if the dog does not have the temperament and character to go with them, then such fine properties are completely wasted.

This imposes some heavy responsibilities upon breeders of the German Shepherd. In the past, the limitations of available stock, the pre-eminence of certain show-winning bloodlines and the tendency to breed 'fashions' have all taken their toll. In the decades immediately after World War II, it was realised that something had to be done to improve the breed. Long before the creation of the WUSV, forward thinking breeders from many countries had begun to look for solutions.

The answer was to return to the homeland whence the German Shepherd had originated, where breed-improvement was, as it always had been, the 'raison d'etre' of the SV organisation.

Thus, by the early 1970s nations had gathered at the invitation of the SV to form a voluntary association of national GSD clubs. The WUSV, as it became known, has been described as an organisation which crosses the barriers of race, language, national cultures and political spheres of influence to unite all peoples with a common love of and interest in the German Shepherd Dog.

This gathering of like-minded people — unique in the dog world — is something of a family affair. All delegates are fired by a common aim: that the German Shepherd Dog, the universal working dog, that can be adapted to perform any feat, must be kept on course and constantly improved.

The German Shepherd is widely used today by the police, armed services and in security work of all kinds; in mountain and avalanche rescue; as guide dogs for the blind, as well as companion dogs ministering to their family charges and protecting them from intruders.

It is the realisation that this precious heritage must not be squandered that has led the majority of GSD enthusiasts all over the world to subscribe to the aims of the WUSV — to be faithful to the Standard — and to endeavour to carry those aims out in practice.

This outlook, coupled with a massive restocking operation of imports from Germany, unprecedented since the early decades of the breed's spread, has resulted in dramatic improvements, so that today the top German Shepherds in many countries are comparable with those seen in Germany, even at the Sieger Show.

THE BREED STANDARD

Characteristics The main characteristics of the GSD are: steadiness of nerves, attentiveness, loyalty, calm self-assurance, alertness and tractability. These characteristics are necessary for a

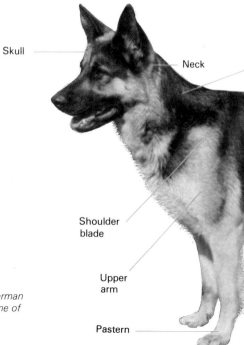

Skull

Neck

Shoulder blade

Upper arm

Pastern

Right: *A photograph of a German Shepherd bitch showing some of the areas and names of conformation.*

versatile working dog. Nervousness, over-aggressiveness and shyness are very serious faults.

General appearance The immediate impression of the GSD is of a dog slightly long in comparison to its height, with a powerful and well-muscled body. The relation between height and length and the position and symmetry of the limbs (angulation) is so interrelated as to enable a far reaching and enduring gait. The coat should be weather-proof. A beautiful appearance is desirable but this is secondary to his usefulness as a working dog. Sexual characteristics must be well defined — ie the masculinity of the male and the femininity of the female must be unmistakable.

A true to type GSD gives an impression of innate strength, intelligence and suppleness, with harmonious proportions and nothing either overdone or lacking. His whole manner should make it perfectly clear that he is sound in mind and body, and has the physical and mental attributes to make him always ready for tireless action as a working dog.

With an abundance of vitality he must be tractable enough to adapt himself to each situation and to carry out his work willingly and with enthusiasm. He must possess the courage and determination to defend himself, his master or his master's possessions, should the need arise. He must be observant, obedient and a pleasant member of the household, quiet in his own environment, especially with children and other animals, and at ease with adults. Overall he should present an harmonious picture of innate nobility, alertness and self-confidence.

Head The head should be proportionate in size to the body without being coarse, too fine or overlong. The overall appearance should be clean cut and fairly broad between the ears.

Forehead — should be only very slightly domed with little or no trace of centre furrow.

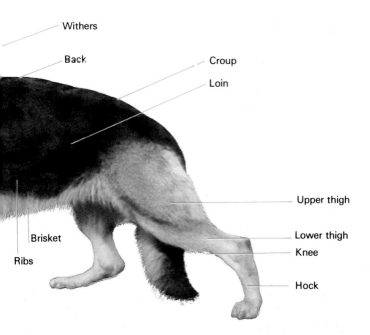

Withers
Back
Croup
Loin
Upper thigh
Brisket
Lower thigh
Ribs
Knee
Hock

Cheeks — should form a very softly rounded curve and should not protrude.

Skull — the skull extends from the ears to the bridge of the nose tapering gradually and evenly, and blending without a too pronounced 'stop' into a wedge-shaped powerful muzzle (the skull is approximately 50% of the whole length of the head). Both top and bottom jaws should be strong and well developed. The width of the skull should correspond approximately to the length. In males the width could be slightly greater and in females slightly less than the length.

Muzzle — should be strong and the lips firm, clean and closing tightly without any flews. The top of the muzzle is straight and almost parallel to the forehead. A muzzle which is too short, blunt, weak, pointed, overlong or lacking in strength is undesirable.

Eyes The eyes are medium-sized, almond-shaped and not protruding. Dark brown eyes are preferred, but eyes of a lighter shade are acceptable provided that the expression is good and the general harmony of the head is not destroyed. The expression should be lively, intelligent and self-assured.

Ears Of medium size, firm in texture, broad at the base, set high, they are carried erect (almost parallel and not pulled inwards), they taper to a point and open towards the front. Tipped ears are faulty. Hanging ears are a very serious fault. During movement the ears may be folded back.

Mouth The jaws must be strongly developed and the teeth healthy, strong and complete. There should be 42 teeth, 20 in the upper jaw, 6 incisors, 2 canines, 8 premolars, 4 molars, and 22 in the lower jaw, 6 incisors, 2 canines, 8 premolars and 6 molars.

The GSD has a scissor bite — ie the incisors in the lower jaw are set behind the incisors in the upper jaw, and thus meet in a scissor grip in which part of the surface of the upper teeth meet and engage part of the surface of the lower teeth.

Neck The neck should be fairly long, strong, with well-developed muscles, free from throatiness (excessive folds of skin at the throat) and carried at an angle of 45° to the horizontal; it is raised when excited and lowered at a fast trot.

Forequarters The shoulder blade should be long, set obliquely (45°) and laid flat to the body. The upper arm should be strong and well muscled and joined to the shoulder blade at a near right angle. The forelegs from the pasterns to the elbows should be straight viewed from any angle and the bones should be oval rather than round. The pasterns should be firm and supple and angulated at approximately 20-23%. Elbows neither tucked in nor turned out. Length of the forelegs should exceed the depth of the chest at a ratio of approximately 55% to 45%.

Body The length of the body should exceed the height at the wither, the correct proportions being as 10 to 9 or 8½. The length is measured from the point of the breast bone to the rear edge of the pelvis.

Over- or under-sized dogs, stunted growth, high-legged dogs and overloaded fronts, too short overall appearance, too light or too heavy in build, steep set limbs or any other feature which detracts from the reach or endurance of the gait, are faulty.

Chest: should be deep (45-48% of the height at the shoulder) but not too broad. The brisket is long and well developed.

Ribs: should be well formed and long, neither barrel-shaped nor too flat; correct rib cage allows free movement of the elbows when the dog is trotting. A too-rounded rib cage will interfere and cause the elbows to be turned out. A too-flat rib cage will lead to the drawing in of the elbows. The desired long ribbing gives a proportionately (relatively) short loin.

Belly: is firm and only slightly

Above: Ch. Gayvilles Dixie, Best of Breed, Crufts 1988. Lovely daughter of prepotent German import: Ch. Meik v.d. Talquelle.

drawn up.

Back: the area between the withers and the croup, straight, strongly developed and not too long. The overall length is not derived from a long back, but is achieved by the correct angle of a well-laid shoulder, correct length of croup and hindquarters. The withers must be long, of good height and well defined. They should join the back in a smooth line without disrupting the flowing top line which should be slightly sloping from the front to the back. Weak, soft and roach backs are undesirable.

Loin: broad, strong and well muscled.

Croup: should be long and gently curving down to the tail (approximately 23°) without disrupting the flowing top line. The ilium and the sacrum form the skeletal basis of the croup. Short, steep or flat croups are undesirable.

Hindquarters The thighs should be broad and well muscled. The upper thigh bone viewed from the side should slope to the slightly longer lower thigh bone. The angulations should correspond approximately with the front angulation without being overangulated. The hock bone is strong and together with the stifle bone should form a firm hock joint. The hindquarters overall must be strong and well muscled to enable the effortless forward propulsion of the whole body. Any tendency towards overangulation of the hindquarters reduces firmness and endurance.

Feet Should be rounded, toes well closed and arched. Pads should be well cushioned and durable. Nails short, strong and dark in colour. Dew-claws are sometimes found on hind-legs; these should be removed 2-3 days after birth.

Gait The GSD is a trotting dog. His sequence of step therefore follows a diagonal pattern in that he always moves the foreleg and the opposite hindleg forward at the same time. To achieve this, his limbs must be in such balance to one another so that he can thrust the hind foot well forward to the midpoint of the body and have an equally long reach with the fore foot without any noticeable change in the back line.

The correct proportion of height to length and corresponding length of limbs will produce a ground-covering stride that travels flat over the ground, giving the impression of effortless movement. With his head thrust forward and a slightly raised tail, a balanced and even trotter displays a flowing line running from the tips of his ears over the neck and back down to the tip of the tail.

The gait should be supple, smooth and long reaching, carrying the body with the minimum of up and down movement, entirely free from stiltiness.

Tail Bushy haired, should reach at least to the hock joint, the ideal length being to the middle of the hock bones. The end is sometimes turned sideways with a slight hook; this is allowed but not desired. When at rest the tail should hang in a slight curve like a sabre. When moving it is raised and the curve is increased, but ideally it should not be higher than the level of the back. A tail that is too short, rolled or curled, or generally carried badly or which is stumpy from birth, is faulty.

Coat

a) The normal coated GSD should carry a thick undercoat and the outer coat should be as dense as possible, made up of straight, hard, close-lying hairs. The hair on the head and ears, front of the legs, paws and toes is short. On the neck it is longer and thicker, on some males forming a slight ruff. The hair grows longer on the back of the legs as far down as the pastern and the stifle, and forms fairly thick trousers on the hindquarters. There is no hard or fast rule for the length of the hair, but short mole-type coats are faulty.

b) In the long-haired GSD the hairs are longer, not always straight and definitely not lying close and flat to the body. They are distinctly longer inside and behind the ears, and on the back of the forelegs and usually at the loins, and form moderate tufts in the ears and profuse feathering on the back of the legs. The trousers are long and thick. The tail is bushy with light feathering underneath. As this type of coat is not so weatherproof as the normal coat it is undesirable.

Below: *Ch. Acresway Gundo. Best male GSD, Crufts 1988. British bred from Canto/Quanto/Mutz lines, and Marko blood.*

c) In the long open-coated GSD the hair is appreciably longer than in the case of type (b) and tends to form a parting along the back, the texture being somewhat silky. If present at all, undercoat is found only at the loins. Dogs with this type of coat are usually narrow-chested, with narrow overlong muzzles. As the weather protection of the dog and his working ability are seriously diminished with this type of coat it is undesirable.

Colour Black or black saddle with tan, or gold to light grey markings. All black, all grey or grey with lighter or brown markings (these are referred to as sables). Small white marks on the chest or very pale colour on inside of legs are permitted but not desirable. The nose in all cases must be black. Light markings on the chest and inside of legs, as well as whitish nails, red tipped nails or wishy-washy faded colour are defined as lacking in pigmentation. Blues, livers, albinos, whites (ie almost pure white dogs with black noses) and near whites are to be rejected.

The undercoat is, except in all-black dogs, grey or fawn in colour.

The colour of the GSD is in itself not important and has no effect on the character of the dog or in its fitness for work and should be a secondary consideration for that reason. The final colour of a young dog can only be ascertained when the outer coat has developed.

Height The ideal height (measured to the highest point of the wither) is 57.5cm for females and 62.5 for males. 2.5cm either above or below the norm is allowed. Any increase in this deviation detracts from the work ability and breeding value of the animal.

Faults Any departure from the foregoing points should be considered a fault and the seriousness with which the fault should be regarded be in exact proportion to its degree.

Note: Male animals must have two apparently normal testicles fully developed into the scrotum.

Below: *Ch. Jacnel Nacale, top British German Shepherd 1987. She gained her championship title in 1986 under SV judges.*

Appendix

Major kennel clubs
Australia Australian National Kennel Council, Royal Show Grounds, Ascot Vale, Victoria (Incorporating: The Canine Association of Western Australia; North Australian Canine Association; The Canine Control Council (Queensland); Canberra Kennel Association; The Kennel Control Council; Kennel Control Council of Tasmania; The RAS Kennel Club; South Australian Canine Association)
Canada Canadian Kennel Club, 2150 Bloor Street West, Toronto M6S 1M8, Ontario
France Societe Centrale Canine, 215 Rue St Denis, 75083 Paris, Cedex 02
Germany Verband für das Deutsche Hundewesen (VDH), Postfach 1390, 46 Dortmund
New Zealand Kennel Club, Private bag, Porirua
South Africa Kennel Union of Southern Africa, 6th FLoor, Bree Castle, 68 Bree Street, Cape Town 8001, S. Africa, PO Box 11280. Vlaeberg 8018
United Kingdom The Kennel Club, 1-4 Clarges Street, London W1Y 8AB
United States of America American Kennel Club, 51 Madison Avenue, New York, NY 10010

Breed clubs
United Kingdom
British Association for German Shepherd Dogs, General Secretary, 55a South Road, Erdington, Birmingham B23 6ED
The German Shepherd Dog Breed Council of Great Britain (representing the majority of breed clubs) Sec, Mrs S. Rankin, 94a Shepherd Hill, Harold Wood, Essex
The German Shepherd Dog League of Great Britain (member club of the WUSV) Hon Sec Mrs J. Ixer, Silverlee, Sparsholt, Winchester, Hants SO21 2NZ
United States
The German Shepherd Dog Club of America Inc, Corresponding Sec: Miss Blanche Beisswenger, 17 West Ivy Lane, Inglewood, New Jersey
West Germany
Verein für Deutsche Schäferhunde (SV) Direktor: C.Lux, Beim Schnarrbrunnen 4-6, D-8900 Augsburg. (Also HQ of the WUSV.)

Bibliography and further reading
The breed
The Complete German Shepherd Dog, Nem & Percy Elliot, Kay & Ward, Kingswood
All about the German Shepherd, M. Pickup, Pelham, London
The Alsatian (German Shepherd Dog), Schwabacher & Gray, Popular Dogs, London
The German Shepherd Dog — 8th Edition — Capt. von Stephanitz, SV Augsburg (1950)
The German Shepherd Dog: its care and training, M. Tidbold, K&R Books, Edlington, Lincs.
The German Shepherd Dog: Its History, Development & Genetics, Dr Malcolm Willis, K&R Books, Edlington, Lincs
The German Shepherd Dog Today, Moses & Strickland, Macmillan, New York (1974)
Modern Bloodlines in the Alsatian, Nem Elliott, Kaye & Ward, London

Training
Heelaway Your Dog, C. Wyant, Canine Publications, Portsmouth
Dog Training my Way, Barbara Woodhouse, Woodhouse, Rickmansworth
Dog Training: Your Pet to Champion, W. Chadwick, Richard Boyes, Stalybridge
Training the Alsatian (German Shepherd Dog), J. Cree, Pelham Books, London
The Working Trial Dog, Peter Lewis, Popular Dogs, London
Nosework for Dogs, J. Cree, Pelham Books, London
Tracking Dog — Theory & Methods, Glen R. Johnson, Arner Publications, Westmoreland, New York

Breed magazines
SV Zeitung, contact breed clubs for address
The German Shepherd Dog National Magazine, Official Journal of the GSD Breed Council of Great Britain, contact breed clubs for address

Yearbooks
GSD League Handbook, details from the League Secretary

German terms found on pedigrees
'a' Zuerk
'A' stamp for hips ie suitable breeding
FH (Fährtenhund)
tracking dog qualification
HGH (Herdengebrauchshund)
qualification for active herding dog
Int. Prüf. Internationale prüfrung
International Working Trials qualification
Jugendsieger (in)
Youth Sieger (in)
Junghundsieger (in)
Young dog Sieger/Young bitch Siegerin
Körklasse 1a/11a
Breed Survey Class 1a or 2a
Lebenzeit
for life (ie breed surveyed)
Sch H1,11,111
'Schutzhund' Tests 1,2 and 3 which include obedience, nosework, agility, and protection work
Sieger
Top dog of the 'Excellent Select' (VA) group at the Sieger Show
Siegerin
Top bitch of the 'Excellent Select' (VA) group at the Sieger Show
SG (Segr Gut)
breed grade 'Very Good'
V (Vorzüglich)
breed grade 'Excellent'
VA (Vorzüglich Auslese)
breed grade 'Excellent Select' (at Sieger Show only)
Vize Sieger(in)
Reserve Sieger(in)

Useful Addresses
The United Kingdom
The Agility Club The Spinney, Aubrey Lane, Redbourn, Hertfordshire AL3 7AN
The Blue Cross Animals Hospital, 1 High Street, Victoria, London SW1V 1QQ
British Small Animals Veterinary Association 7 Mansfield Street, London
British Veterinary Association 7 Mansfield Street, London W1M 0AT
The Guide Dogs for the Blind Association 9-11 Park Street, Windsor, Berkshire SL4 1JR
National Canine Defence League 1 Pratt Mews, London NW1 0AD
People's Dispensary for Sick Animals PDSA House, South Street, Dorking, Surrey
The Royal Society for the Prevention of Cruelty to Animals RSPCA Headquarters, Causeway, Horsham, Sussex RH12 1HG
United States of America
American Animal Hospital Association 3612 East Jefferson, South Bend, Indiana 46615
American Humane Association (incorporating The Hearing Dog Association) 5351 Roslyn, Denver, Colorado 80201
American Society for the Prevention of Cruelty to Animals 441 East 92nd Street, New York, New York 10028
American Veterinary Medical Association 930 North Meacham Road, Schaumburg, Illinois 60196
Animal Welfare Institute PO Box 3650, Washington D.C. 20007
Guide Dogs for the Blind PO Box 1200, San Rafael, California 94902
The Humane Society of the United States 2100 L Street, N.W., Washington D.C. 20037
Leader Dogs for the Blind 1039 South Rochester Road, Rochester, Michigan 48063
Orthopaedic Foundation for Animals 817 Virginia Avenue, Columbia, Missouri 65201
Owner Handler Association of America 583 Knoll Court, Seaford, New York 11783

Glossary of dog terminology

AKC: American Kennel Club
Angulation: Angle formed by the bones, mainly the shoulder, forearm, stifle and hock.
Anorchid: Male animal without testicles.
Anus: Anterior opening under the tail.
Backline: Topline of dog from neck to tail.
Bite: The position of the teeth when the mouth is shut.
Bitch: Female dog.
Breastbone: Bone running down the middle of the chest, to which all but the floating ribs are attached; sternum.
Breeder: Someone who breeds dogs.
Brisket: The forepart of the body below the chest between the forelegs.
Brood bitch: Female used for breeding.
Bull neck: A heavy neck, well-muscled.
Canine: Animal of the genus canis which includes dogs, foxes, wolves and jackals.
Canines: The four large teeth in the front of the mouth, two upper and two lower next to incisors.
Carpals: Bones of the pastern joints.
Castrate: To surgically remove the testes of a male.
Cow-hocked: Hocks turned inwards.
Croup: The rear part of the back above the hind legs.
Crown: The highest part of the head: the top of the skull.
Cryptorchid: A male dog with neither testicle descended.
Cull: To eliminate unwanted puppies.
Dam: Mother of the puppies.
Dew claw: Extra claw on the inside lower portion of legs.
Elbow: The joint between the upper arm and forearm.
Femur: The large heavy bone of the thigh between the pelvis and stifle joint.
Flank: Side of the body between the last rib and the hip.
Forearm: Front leg between elbow and pastern.
Foreface: Front part of the head before the eyes; the muzzle.
Handler: A person who handles (shows) a dog at dog shows, field trials or obedience tests.
Hare foot: A long narrow foot.
Haw: A third eyelid at the inside corner of the eye.
Heat: An alternative word for 'season' in bitches.
Heel: Command by handler to keep the dog close to his heel.
Heel free: Command whereby the dog must walk to heel without a lead.
Height: Vertical measurements from withers to ground.
Hip dysplasia: Malformation of the ball of the hip joint.
Hock: Lower joint of the hind-legs.
Hucklebones: Top of the hip bones.
Humerus: Bone of the upper arm.
In-breeding: The mating of closely related dogs of the same standard.
Incisors: Upper and lower front teeth between the canines.
Ischium: Hipbone.
In season: On heat, ready for mating.
Inter-breeding: The breeding together of different varieties.
Jowls: Flesh of lips and jaws.
Level bite: The upper and lower teeth edge to edge.
Line breeding: The mating of related dogs within a line or family to a common ancestor, ie dog to grand-dam or bitch to grand-sire.
Litter: The pups from one whelping.
Loin: Either side of the vertebrae column between the last rib and hip bone.

Mate: The sex act between the dog and bitch.
Milk teeth: First teeth. (Puppies lose these at four to six months.)
Molars: Rear teeth.
Monorchid: A male animal with only one testicle in the scrotum.
Muzzle: The head in front of the eyes, including nose, nostril and jaws.
Nose: The ability to scent.
Occiput: The rear of the skull.
Oestrum: The period during which a bitch has her menstrual flow and can be mated.
Out-crossing: The mating of unrelated individuals of the same breed.
Overshot: Front teeth (incisors) of the upper jaw overlap and do not touch the teeth of the lower jaw.
Pads: The tough, cushioned soles of the feet.
Paper foot: A flat foot with thin pads.
Pastern: Foreleg between the carpus and the digits.
Patella: Knee cap composed of cartilage at the stifle joint.
Pedigree: The written record of the names of a dog's ancestors.
Pelvis: Set of bones attached to the end of the spinal column.
Pigeon-toed: With toes pointing in.
Police dog: A dog trained for police work (often the German Shepherd Dog).
Puppy: A dog up to 12 months of age.
Quarters: The two hindlegs.
Scapula: The shoulder blade.
Scissor bite: The outside of the lower incisors touches the inner side of the upper incisors.
Second thigh: The part of the hindquarters from stifle to hock.
Seeing eye dog: A guide dog for the blind (in the USA).
Set on: Insertion or attachment of tail or ears.
Set up: Posed so as to make the most of the dog's appearance for the show ring.
Sire: A dog's male parent.
Soft-mouthed: Able to carry retrieved game in the mouth without damaging it.
Spay: To surgically remove the ovaries to prevent conception.
Splay feet: Feet with toes spread wide.
Standard: The standard of perfection for a breed.
Sternum: The brisket or breast bone.
Stifle: The hindlegs above the hock.
Stop: Indentation between the eyes.
Stud: Male used for breeding.
Tail set: How the base of the tail sets on the rump.
Thigh: Hindquarters from hip to stifle.
Throatiness: An excess of loose skin under the throat.
Topline: The dog's outline from just behind the withers to the tail set.
Type: The characteristic qualities distinguishing a breed; the embodiment of the standards essentials.
Under-coat: The soft, furry wool beneath the outer hair, giving protection against cold and wet.
Undershot: The front teeth of the lower jaw projecting or overlapping the front teeth of the upper jaw.
Upper arm: The humerus or bone of the foreleg between shoulder blade and the forearm.
Vent: The anal opening.
Whelp: The act of giving birth.
Withers: The highest point of the shoulders just behind the neck.
Wrymouth: Mouth in which the lower jaw does not line up with the upper.